The Age of Abundance

AI and the Future of Work, Wealth, and Purpose

The Age of Abundance Series
Book 1

Leandro Maya

Evergreen Nexus

ISBN: 979-8-9950295-0-2

Published by Evergreen Nexus LLC

First Edition, 2026

DISCLAIMER

The views and opinions expressed in this book are those of the author and do not necessarily reflect the official policy or position of any organization, company, or institution with which the author has been associated. This book is intended for informational purposes only and should not be construed as professional financial, legal, or career advice. Readers should consult appropriate professionals for specific guidance related to their individual circumstances.

For speaking inquiries, media requests, or corporate consulting:

hello@leandromaya.com

www.leandromaya.com

Acknowledgments

This book would not exist without the support, wisdom, and patience of many people.

First and foremost, to my wife Laura and our children, Luca and Lila: Thank you for your endless patience during the countless hours I spent writing, researching, and revising. You are not only my inspiration, but you are also my reason. Every word in this book was written with the hope of helping build a better future for you.

To my family and friends: You are the ones who listened patiently as I tested ideas, challenged assumptions, and talked endlessly about AI, the future of work, and the future of money. Your questions helped me clarify my thinking. Your skepticism made my arguments stronger. And your encouragement convinced me this was a topic worth exploring deeply. Thank you for believing this book mattered before it existed.

To my colleagues at Circle, Facebook, Apple, DLL, and PwC: Working alongside you gave me a front-row seat to how technology and innovation reshape industries and economies. The insights I gained from our conversations, projects, and shared challenges form the foundation of this book. Thank you for teaching me to think critically about the future we're building.

I should also note that I used AI tools throughout the writing process, including Claude, ChatGPT, and Grok. They helped me research unfamiliar domains, pressure-test arguments, and refine drafts. It feels fitting that a book about the automation era was written with the help of the tools it describes. The ideas, the arguments, and the judgments are mine. The mistakes are too.

Finally, to you, the reader: Thank you for caring about the future enough to think seriously about it. The conversations we need to have about automation, purpose, and abundance won't happen in government offices or corporate boardrooms alone. They'll happen in living rooms, coffee shops, and dinner tables. Wherever people gather to ask hard questions about what comes next. By reading this book, you're part of that conversation. And that matters more than you know.

Introduction

This isn't the book I expected to write.

The idea started, honestly, at the dinner table. My wife Laura and I were having one of those ordinary weeknight meals with our kids, Lila and Luca, when Lila, who was ten at the time, asked me what I actually do for work. I gave her the simplified version: something about helping people send money around the world. She thought about it for a second, looked at me with the unnerving directness only a child can manage, and said, "Why can't a computer just do that?"

Laura laughed. Luca, who was thirteen, smiled but said nothing. But that night, after the kids were in bed, I couldn't stop thinking about it. Because the honest answer to Lila's question, the one I didn't give a ten-year-old, was: yes. Increasingly, it can.

And not just what I do. What millions of people do.

I should be clear from the start: I'm not a roboticist, economist, or Silicon Valley insider. I haven't built autonomous systems or published papers on labor markets. I don't have insider access to the labs where the future is being assembled.

What I have is something different, and in some ways, more useful for this conversation. I'm an observer who's spent years unable to stop thinking about what happens next. Not as science fiction. Not as speculation. As something that increasingly feels inevitable once you see how all the pieces fit together.

And here's what makes this moment different from every other time someone has predicted a technological revolution: the future isn't coming anymore. It's here.

In early 2026, the humanoid robotics industry crossed a threshold that most people outside the industry haven't fully registered. Multiple companies, not one, but several, backed by billions of dollars and some of the most sophisticated engineering organizations on Earth, moved humanoid robots from research labs into early production. Not prototypes for demonstrations. Production models, designed for real work in real environments.

Across the United States, China, Japan, and Europe, companies began deploying humanoid robots in commercial warehouses and manufacturing facilities. Platforms that had been viral video curiosities a few years earlier advanced into genuine industrial tools. Several companies announced humanoid platforms at price points that would have seemed absurd three years earlier. At least one major automaker pushed its humanoid program toward manufacturing scale on its own assembly lines.

No single company's timeline matters. What matters is the convergence: when multiple well-funded organizations pursue the same goal simultaneously, at least one will succeed. And once one demonstrates commercial viability, competitive pressure drags everyone else forward. The humanoid moment didn't arrive because of any single genius or company. It arrived because the economics became undeniable.

While we've been debating what might happen someday, that someday has arrived.

This book exists because I kept noticing the same gap in nearly every conversation about AI, automation, and what's coming next. People were talking about fragments: job displacement over here, technological capability over there, inequality in one corner, abundance in another, geopolitics somewhere else. Each perspective was valid. Each contained truth. But they rarely connected into a coherent picture of the entire transformation. Not just technologically, but socially, economically, and psychologically.

That's what I've tried to do here. To see the whole shape of the thing.

What This Book Is

This book is not a technical research paper. It is a strategic synthesis: connecting technology, economics, labor, energy, geopolitics, and human meaning into one coherent map of what comes next.

I'm not presenting groundbreaking studies or novel data. I'm drawing connections between trends that are already visible: robots working in warehouses, AI systems writing code, the changing economics of manufacturing, the evolution of energy systems, the transformation of healthcare, the restructuring of global supply chains.

My role here isn't expert. It's observer.

I'm someone who's spent years reading, thinking, and asking: what happens when you take all of these trends seriously and follow them to their logical endpoints? What does the world look like when intelligence becomes cheap? When physical labor becomes automated? When the fundamental economics of production change?

This book is also an exercise in clarity. The conversation around AI and automation is often captured by two extremes: utopian visions that ignore disruption, or dystopian warnings that ignore possibility. The truth, I believe, lives in neither extreme. The automation era isn't a story of inevitable paradise or unavoidable catastrophe. It's a story of choices. Choices that will determine whether the coming decades deliver unprecedented abundance or deepen existing fractures.

I've tried to write something balanced. Something that takes both promise and peril seriously. Something that's honest about what we don't know while being clear about what we can see.

What This Book Is Not

This isn't a technical manual. If you're looking for detailed explanations of how transformer architectures work or how robotic grasping systems function, this isn't that book. There are excellent resources for that, written by people far more qualified than I am.

This isn't an academic treatise. There are no footnotes citing hundreds of papers. There are no formulas or statistical models. I'm not trying to convince a peer review board. I'm trying to help people understand what's happening and why it matters.

This isn't prophecy. I don't claim to know exactly when specific technologies will become mainstream, which companies will dominate, or how governments will respond. The future isn't written yet, and anyone who claims perfect foresight should be viewed skeptically, including me.

What I'm offering is a framework, a way of thinking about what may be coming and why it matters. A lens for understanding the transformation that's already underway.

Why I Wrote This

I grew up in Brazil, in a country where economic instability wasn't something you read about. It was something you lived. My parents navigated hyperinflation, currency crises, and the kind of uncertainty that makes you acutely aware of how fragile economic systems really are. That experience shaped me in ways I didn't fully appreciate until I started writing this book.

Because this book is, at its core, about a different kind of economic instability. Not the kind caused by bad monetary policy or political dysfunction. The kind caused by a structural shift so deep that the rules themselves change.

Introduction

I wrote this book because I believe we're living through one of
the most important transitions in human history, and most
people don't yet understand how profound it will be.

Not because the technology is magical.

Because the economics are changing.

For most of human history, the limiting factor in nearly
everything was human labor and human attention. Think
about any major project: building the pyramids, constructing
the Interstate Highway System, manufacturing automobiles,
processing financial transactions. What did they all require?
People. Lots of people.

If you wanted more output, you needed more workers. More
hands in factories. More drivers on roads. More clerks in
offices. More nurses in hospitals. This was true in ancient
Egypt, and it remained true through most of the twentieth
century.

The automation era changes that equation fundamentally.

It creates systems where productivity can grow without
proportional growth in employment. Where intelligence
becomes cheap and scalable. Where physical tasks, building,
moving, delivering, assembling, can be done by machines that
don't tire, don't demand wages, and improve with every
iteration.

Let me give you a concrete example from right now, not some
distant future.

As I write this in February 2026, humanoid robots are no
longer a laboratory curiosity. They are entering production
across multiple companies and countries. They stand roughly

human height, weigh roughly human weight, and have hands capable of the kind of fine motor tasks, sorting, assembling, handling delicate objects, that we long assumed required human dexterity.

The projected prices put them within range of what a small business owner might pay for a piece of equipment, not what a research institution budgets for a prototype.

This isn't a small shift. This is structural. And it will reshape everything: work, income, education, healthcare, politics, global power, and the fundamental question of what it means to live a meaningful life when survival no longer requires labor.

I wrote this book because I wanted to think through those implications seriously, not just for economists or policymakers, but for anyone trying to understand the world their children will inherit.

I wrote it, frankly, because of Lila and Luca. Because the world they'll grow up in will look nothing like the one I navigated. And I wanted to understand that world well enough to help them prepare for it.

The Moment We're In

Here's what makes 2026 different from 2020, or 2015, or any previous year where people predicted transformative change:

The technology has matured. AI systems can now write code, diagnose diseases, drive vehicles, understand images, generate art, and conduct conversations that feel genuinely intelligent. Humanoid robots from at least half a dozen companies can navigate human environments and manipulate objects with increasing dexterity. These aren't parlor tricks anymore. They're economically viable alternatives to human labor.

The economics have shifted. As of early 2026, most software developers use AI coding tools regularly. Companies report that AI generates a significant and growing share of their code. The pattern is the same across industries: tasks that required rooms full of professionals a decade ago now require a fraction of that headcount. Not because the professionals were bad at their jobs, because the tools became extraordinarily good.

The adoption curve has accelerated. What seemed like distant possibilities in 2023 became working prototypes in 2024, pilot programs in 2025, and are moving toward production scale in 2026. The pace isn't linear. It's exponential.

I saw this firsthand in my own career. At Circle, I watched the financial infrastructure of the future being built in real time: programmable money, stablecoins settling billions in transactions, systems that operated at a speed and scale that made traditional banking look like it was running on paper ledgers. Before that, at Apple and Meta, I saw how quickly technology platforms could reshape entire industries. Not over decades. Over quarters.

This matters because transformative technology doesn't change the world when it becomes impressive. It changes the world when it becomes cheaper than the old way.

And we've reached that inflection point.

How to Read This Book

This book is structured to build understanding progressively.

The early chapters establish what's changing right now: the technological and economic foundations, why it's changing now, and what makes this moment different from previous waves of automation.

The middle chapters explore implications: what happens to work, to income systems, to global trade, to energy, to money, to education when machines can do what humans do, only cheaper and more reliably.

The later chapters address deeper questions: purpose, longevity, timelines, and what the best version of this future might look like.

You can read this book straight through, or you can jump to the chapters that interest you most. Each chapter is designed to stand on its own while contributing to the larger argument.

My hope is that you'll finish this book with a clearer sense of what's coming, not to fear it, but to think seriously about how we might shape it.

A Note on Uncertainty

I should be honest about what I don't know.

I don't know exactly when autonomous vehicles will dominate transportation. I don't know which countries will adopt automation fastest, which industries will resist longest, or how social movements will respond. I don't know whether the transition will be smooth or chaotic, whether abundance will be widely shared or concentrated, whether people will find new sources of meaning or struggle with purposelessness.

I could be wrong about the timeline. In fact, history suggests I probably am, but not in the way you might think. Technology predictions are almost always wrong about timing, but they tend to err in both directions. Some things arrive faster than expected. Smartphones went from niche products to ubiquity in less than a decade. AI language models became genuinely useful far sooner than most experts predicted. Others take longer: we've been promised fusion energy and flying cars for generations.

What rarely happens is that transformative technologies just don't arrive at all.

Humanoid robots are here. They're entering production across companies in the United States, China, Japan, and Europe. The question isn't whether they'll transform labor markets, but how fast and how disruptively. Whether that transformation takes five years or fifteen years matters enormously for planning and adaptation, but either timeline represents a fundamental restructuring of how human society works.

What I do believe is this: the direction is clear, even if the timeline isn't.

The incentives are aligning. The technology is maturing. The economic logic is becoming undeniable. The world is reaching a level of complexity where automation stops being optional and becomes structural.

The question isn't whether this era is coming.

The question is what we do with it.

An Invitation

A few months before I finished this manuscript, I was visiting family in Garopaba, a small beach town in southern Brazil where I'm building a house. One evening, my dad and I were sitting on the porch watching the sun set over the Atlantic. He asked what the book was about. I gave him the short version: machines are going to do most of the work humans do today, and we need to figure out what that means for everyone.

He was quiet for a long time. Then he said something I keep coming back to: "That sounds like it could be the best thing that ever happened, or the worst. Depends on who's making the decisions."

He's right. And that's why this book isn't meant to be the final word on anything. It's meant to be a starting point, for thought, for conversation, for deeper exploration.

If you finish this book thinking differently about the future, whether you agree with my perspective or not, then it has succeeded. Because the automation era won't be decided by experts alone. It will be shaped by everyone who takes the time to understand what's happening and asks: what kind of world do we want to build?

That question matters more than any algorithm.

Let's begin.

Chapter 1
The Turning Point

On a Wednesday morning in November 2025, a warehouse in Nevada held a meeting that nobody outside the company noticed. The operations manager stood in front of thirty-seven night-shift workers and delivered news that felt both shocking and inevitable: their jobs would end in six months. Not because of poor performance. Not because the warehouse was closing. Because the company had decided to automate the entire night operation.

The robots that would replace them, squat, wheeled machines that looked nothing like the sci-fi humanoids from movies, could work around the clock without breaks, didn't require health insurance or overtime pay, and made fewer mistakes sorting packages. The math was brutal and simple: the machines would pay for themselves in less than two years. Every competitor was making the same move. The company had no choice.

None of those workers made the news. There were no protests, no viral videos, no dramatic headlines. Just thirty-seven people, with families, mortgages, car payments, learning that the economy had stopped needing what they were offering.

This is how the future actually arrives. Not with spectacle, but with spreadsheets. Not through revolution, but through quiet, rational, economically inevitable decisions made in unremarkable conference rooms across the world.

I know this story because versions of it have been reaching me for years, from colleagues, from industry contacts, from friends managing operations in logistics and manufacturing and financial services. Each story is different in its details. Each is identical in its structure. A team gets called together. A decision gets announced. The economics are explained. And the room goes quiet.

The Pattern Becomes Undeniable

That warehouse wasn't unique. It was a data point in a pattern that's accelerating across the entire economy.

In early 2024, a radiologist noticed something unsettling. The AI system her hospital had installed to pre-screen chest X-rays wasn't just flagging obvious problems, it was catching subtle patterns she might have missed. Lung nodules barely visible to the human eye. Early signs of heart failure in the vascular shadows. The AI had been trained on millions of images and could compare any new scan against that vast library in seconds.

She's still employed. Still essential for complex cases and final decisions. But the hospital that used to need six radiologists for routine screenings now needs three. The other positions weren't eliminated, they just weren't replaced when people retired or moved on. The work still gets done. It just requires fewer humans.

Meanwhile, at a law firm, junior associates who once spent their first two years reviewing contracts for due diligence now watch as AI systems do the same work in hours instead of weeks. The associates still have jobs, they've been promoted to more strategic work earlier than they would have been a decade ago. But the firm that used to hire twelve new graduates each year now hires four.

And at a startup that would have hired twenty engineers to build their product in 2020, the 2025 team is seven people. The other thirteen positions aren't needed anymore. AI coding tools generate the routine code, handle the boilerplate, write the tests, and catch the bugs. The humans do the creative architecture and strategic decisions, but there's just less human labor required overall.

These aren't stories about mass unemployment. They're stories about something more subtle and potentially more disruptive: the economy learning to produce more with less. Each example represents the same economic equation shifting.

And when you see the same pattern across warehouses, hospitals, law firms, software companies, manufacturing plants, customer service centers, and logistics operations, you're not looking at isolated incidents. You're looking at a turning point.

A Revolution That Doesn't Look Like a Revolution

Most revolutions arrive with spectacle. Wars, elections, movements, leaders, slogans. The automation era is different. It arrives quietly, through decisions that feel mundane in the moment.

A procurement manager approves a purchase order for new warehouse equipment. A hospital administrator signs off on an AI diagnostic system. A law firm partners with a legal tech company. A factory installs its fifth generation of robotic assembly equipment. None of these decisions make headlines. Each one is rational, defensible, economically sound.

But add them up across thousands of companies and millions of decisions, and you get a transformation.

It won't feel like a revolution at first. It'll feel like progress. Faster delivery. Smoother service. Smarter assistants. Fewer errors. Better quality. Lower costs. And, almost as an afterthought, slightly fewer jobs.

That's why it'll be underestimated. The first stage won't look like disruption. It'll look like efficiency. Like the natural evolution of business. Like common sense.

The future rarely arrives in a way that feels dramatic to the people living inside it. It arrives in a way that feels rational. Obvious. Necessary.

I've watched this happen from inside financial services. At Circle, the tools we use today would have been unimaginable five years ago. Tasks that once required a junior analyst working for a week now take a senior person with AI assistance an afternoon. Nobody held a meeting to announce that shift. It just accumulated, one tool at a time, one workflow at a time, until the before and after became unrecognizable. The same team produces dramatically more than it could three years ago. Not because the people got smarter, but because the tools got extraordinarily good. And when you see that pattern inside your own company, you start to understand what it means when it spreads across every industry simultaneously.

The Central Question of the Century

Every era has a defining question. The question that shapes politics, culture, and the structure of daily life.

The twentieth century wrestled with how to organize industrial societies: capitalism versus communism, democracy versus authoritarianism, the power to destroy versus the power to rebuild. Those debates shaped everything from elections to education systems to where people lived and how they worked.

The twenty-first century's defining question is emerging now, and it's deeper than most people realize:

What happens when labor is no longer scarce?

That sounds technical. It isn't. It's everything.

Because for all of human history, scarcity shaped civilization. Scarcity of food determined where people settled. Scarcity of clean water determined which cities thrived. Scarcity of arable land determined wars and migrations. Scarcity of skilled labor determined social hierarchies and economic power.

But most fundamentally, scarcity of labor forced societies to organize themselves around work. Work became how people earned the right to participate in the economy. Work became the distribution system for income. Work became identity, status, structure, purpose.

Not as a moral judgment, but as an economic necessity: if you wanted to eat, you had to contribute something the market valued. If society needed more production, it needed more workers. The entire social contract was built on that foundation.

Growing up in Brazil, I saw what happens when that contract frays even slightly. My parents' generation lived through economic crises where the system stopped delivering on its basic promise: work hard, and life gets better. When that promise breaks, when the contract between effort and reward stops functioning, people don't just lose income. They lose faith in the structure itself. The automation era threatens a deeper version of that same rupture, not through policy failure or currency collapse, but through a structural shift in what labor is worth.

The automation era challenges that arrangement. And when you challenge a foundational assumption of civilization, everything downstream begins to shift.

Why This Time Is Different

I know what some readers are thinking: we've heard this before.

And you'd be right to be skeptical. Every generation has been told machines would change everything. Textile workers smashed machinery in the 1810s, convinced mechanization would destroy their livelihoods. In the 1960s, economists warned that automation would create mass unemployment. In the 1990s, people feared computers would eliminate office jobs.

And yet, people still work. New industries emerged. The economy adapted. Life went on.

So why should we believe it's different this time?

Because this is the first wave of automation that attacks both halves of human economic value simultaneously.

Previous revolutions followed a predictable pattern. Machines replaced muscle, humans moved to brain work. The Industrial Revolution eliminated agricultural labor, but it created factory jobs, clerical positions, management roles. The computer revolution eliminated typing pools and calculation work, but it created programming, data analysis, knowledge work.

Each wave pushed humans up the cognitive ladder. The assumption was there would always be another rung, some tasks that required uniquely human intelligence, creativity, or judgment.

This wave is different. AI automates cognition while robotics automates physical tasks. Both ladders are being climbed simultaneously.

That doesn't mean humans become irrelevant. We're not heading toward a world where machines do literally everything. But we are heading toward a world where the structure of the economy fundamentally changes. Where growth and employment decouple. Where productivity increases while the number of people needed to generate that productivity decreases.

Consider what's happened in software development alone. Just five years ago, if a company wanted to build a mobile app, they needed a team: frontend developers, backend developers, database specialists, QA engineers, DevOps people. Each role required years of specialized training. Today, a single competent developer using AI coding tools can do what required a team of five in 2020. The AI writes the boilerplate code, suggests solutions to common problems, generates tests, catches bugs, and even handles deployment pipelines. The human still makes the architectural decisions and handles the creative problem-solving, but the sheer volume of human labor required has dropped dramatically.

And software is supposed to be the safe industry, the place people were told to retrain for when their factory jobs disappeared.

The Moment Economics Become Destiny

Here's what makes this moment irreversible: it's not about technology anymore. It's about economics.

Technology becomes transformative when it becomes cheaper than the old way. Not when it becomes impressive. Not when it becomes possible. When it becomes inevitable.

Consider grocery store cleaning. A floor-scrubbing robot now costs roughly what a single year of a human cleaner's wages and benefits would run, and it works continuously, never complains, and gets better with software updates. The robot pays for itself in less than a year. After that, it's nearly pure savings.

Now multiply that calculation across every grocery chain, every warehouse, every factory, every hospital, every office building. The economic logic is relentless and identical: automation is cheaper.

And here's the critical point: once your competitors automate, you have to automate too. Not because you want to. Because you'll be undercut on price, outperformed on speed, and outlasted on consistency.

This is why I'm confident about the direction even if I'm uncertain about the timeline. The economic incentives are aligning in a way that makes automation not just attractive but compulsory.

The automation era isn't primarily a technological revolution. It's an economic inevitability. The technology is only the enabler. The driver is cost structure. And cost structure always wins.

How Change Actually Arrives

If you're imagining a sudden transformation, one day the world looks normal, the next day it's unrecognizable, that's not how it works.

Real change is uneven. It arrives in pockets. It starts in places most people don't see.

Right now, the transformation is concentrated in warehouses, factories, logistics hubs, data centers, corporate back offices.

The infrastructure of the economy is changing first, quietly, out of sight. Most people don't work in these places, so they don't see it happening.

But the pattern is already clear. A decade ago, a large distribution warehouse might have employed over a thousand people. Today, a comparable facility handles more volume with a fraction of that headcount. The workers who remain are more specialized, maintaining robots, handling exceptions, managing the system. But the raw number of humans required to move the same volume of goods has dropped sharply.

And those patterns spread. First through logistics. Then manufacturing. Then transportation. Then retail. Then healthcare. Then services.

Adoption curves don't move linearly. They move like compound interest. Slow at first, when the technology is expensive and limited. Then faster, as costs drop and capabilities improve. Then exponential, as network effects and competitive pressure accelerate deployment.

Think about smartphones. In 2007, they were luxury items for business travelers and early adopters. By 2010, they were common among professionals. By 2015, everybody had one. The technology didn't change dramatically over those eight years. What changed was cost, infrastructure, and network effects.

We're in the middle of that curve right now with automation. Somewhere between 2010 and 2015 in the smartphone analogy. It's not everywhere yet. But it's not rare anymore either. And the acceleration is about to become undeniable.

When the Job Ladder Breaks

The most concerning aspect isn't that jobs disappear overnight. It's that the entry points close.

Think about how careers used to work. You started at the bottom. You learned on the job. You made mistakes, got better, developed expertise, moved up. The first job might not have been glamorous, but it was a foothold. A way in.

That's what's disappearing first.

Law firms don't need as many junior associates to review documents anymore, AI does that. Accounting firms don't need entry-level staff to reconcile spreadsheets, software handles it. Warehouses don't need people to move inventory between stations, robots do that. Software companies don't need junior developers to write boilerplate code, AI generates it.

The senior positions might remain for now. But how do you become a senior anything without ever being a junior? How do you build expertise without somewhere to start?

This is what I mean by the job ladder breaking. It's not that every rung disappears. It's that the bottom rungs, the entry points, the training positions, the learn-while-you-work roles, vanish first. And without those, the whole pathway becomes inaccessible.

I think about this when I look at Luca, who is sixteen and already planning a path toward medicine. The ladder he's imagining, university, medical school, residency, practice, still exists today. But how much of it will look the same by the time he's climbing it? If AI can already outperform radiologists on routine screenings, what does a radiology residency look like in 2035? If AI systems can synthesize patient histories faster than any intern, where does clinical training begin? The ladder isn't gone. But the rungs are shifting under his feet before he's even stepped on them.

The Social Contract Under Pressure

For centuries, the deal was simple and brutal: work, and you earn the right to live. It wasn't always fair. It excluded many people. It exploited some. But it was functional.

The wage system did more than pay people. It distributed purchasing power throughout society. It created a feedback loop: people worked, earned wages, bought things, companies grew, hired more people. The cycle sustained itself.

It wasn't perfect. It created inequality. It left people behind. But it was stable enough to build modern civilization around. It funded the middle class. It made mass consumption possible. It gave people a clear framework for understanding their economic role.

The automation era breaks that loop.

Not because people stop wanting to work. But because the economy stops needing as many people to produce the same output, or even greater output.

Productivity keeps rising. Goods get cheaper. Services improve. GDP grows. But the connection between economic growth and job creation weakens. Wealth gets created, but the distribution mechanism, wages in exchange for labor, becomes less reliable.

And when that happens, society faces what might be the most important political question of the century: if machines produce the wealth, how do humans receive income?

That's not ideology. That's mechanics. And we're going to have to answer it.

Beyond Economics: The Purpose Problem

If this were only about money, it would still be enormous. But there's something deeper happening.

Work has never been just about income. It's been about structure, identity, status, purpose. It's given people a reason to wake up in the morning, a place to go, colleagues to interact with, skills to develop, contributions to make.

We introduce ourselves by what we do. I'm a teacher. I'm an engineer. I'm a nurse. Our work becomes our identity. Our professional achievements become our status markers. Our daily routines center around work schedules.

These aren't luxuries. They're psychological needs that have been bundled with employment for so long that we've stopped seeing them as separate things.

So, when traditional employment weakens, when the economy needs fewer workers to produce the same output, we're not just facing an economic adjustment. We're facing an existential question:

What do we do with our lives when survival no longer requires labor?

Some people will thrive in that world. They'll pursue art, learning, community building, creative projects they never had time for. They'll find meaning outside economic necessity.

Others will struggle. Not everyone has hobbies that fulfill the need for purpose. Not everyone wants to be their own source of meaning. For many people, the structure of work provided something irreplaceable: a clear role, a place to belong, a reason to matter.

This is the question that most discussions of automation avoid, because it's uncomfortable, because it's not technical, because it can't be solved with a white paper or a product launch.

But it's real. And it will matter more than any algorithm.

What Comes Next

We're at a turning point. Not because the technology is magical, but because the economics have aligned in a way that makes automation inevitable rather than optional.

The transformation won't be instant. It won't be uniform. Some industries will automate faster than others. Some jobs will disappear quickly, others will persist for decades. Some regions will embrace the change, others will resist.

But the direction is clear. The incentives are aligned. The technology is maturing. And the competitive pressures are mounting.

The question isn't whether this era is coming. The question is what we do with it. How we manage the transition. How we distribute the abundance. How we preserve human dignity when economic productivity no longer requires most humans.

That's what the rest of this book explores, not just the technology, but the implications. The workforce changes, the distribution challenges, the geopolitical shifts, the energy transformation, the questions about purpose and meaning.

But here's what makes this era different from every previous disruption: the destination is abundance, not scarcity.

The automation era isn't ultimately about what we lose. It's about what becomes possible. It's about problems that were unsolvable becoming solved. Diseases that were incurable becoming treatable. Energy that was expensive becoming cheap. Goods that were luxuries becoming accessible to billions.

The challenge isn't that we won't have enough. The challenge is that we'll have more than enough, and we'll need to redesign how we distribute it. That's a fundamentally different problem than humanity has ever faced.

The next chapters explore the disruption, because understanding the disruption is essential to navigating it. But never forget: the disruption is the transition, not the destination. The destination is a world where scarcity is optional, where survival is guaranteed, where humans are finally free to pursue meaning rather than mere existence.

That world is what we're building. Whether we build it well or poorly, that's what this book is about.

Chapter 2
The Robot Revolution Is Physical

If Chapter 1 was about understanding the turning point, this chapter is where we land on solid ground. Because the automation era isn't ultimately a story about software or algorithms running in the cloud. It's a story about the physical world.

It's about things moving. Things being built. Things being cleaned. Things being delivered. Things being manufactured. Things being cared for.

The modern economy isn't made of ideas. It's made of operations. And for most of human history, operations required humans. That was the limitation. That was the anchor. That was the reason labor remained central to every economic calculation.

Artificial intelligence changes thought. Robotics changes reality.

And the moment robotics becomes scalable is the moment

the future stops being a concept and becomes infrastructure. That moment is happening right now.

I remember the exact afternoon I understood this viscerally, not just intellectually. I was watching a demonstration video of a humanoid robot, one of the newer models from a company I'd been tracking, and it picked up an egg without breaking it. That sounds trivial. It's not. If you've spent any time around industrial robotics, you know that the gap between "lift a car engine" and "pick up an egg" is the entire history of the field. Brute force was solved decades ago. Delicacy is what separates a machine from a replacement for human hands. And watching that egg stay intact, I thought: this changes everything. Not next decade. Now.

The Humanoid Breakthrough

For years, robotics experts rolled their eyes at humanoid robots. They were seen as gimmicks, marketing stunts, impractical designs that prioritized looking futuristic over being functional. Why build a machine shaped like a human when you could design specialized machines for specific tasks?

The answer turned out to be simpler than anyone expected: because the entire human world is designed for humans. Doorways are human-sized. Stairs are human-scaled. Tools are human-gripped. Workspaces are human-organized. If you build a machine that can navigate human environments and use human tools, you don't need to redesign everything else. The robot can work in factories, warehouses, offices, hospitals, and homes without requiring billions of dollars in infrastructure changes.

That was the insight. And by early 2026, it had moved from insight to manufacturing intent across an entire industry.

The convergence is what makes this moment different from previous robotics hype cycles. This isn't one visionary company making bold promises. It's a global race. In the United States, at least half a dozen well-funded companies are building humanoid platforms, backed by some of the largest technology investors on Earth. In China, multiple companies have announced humanoid robots at price points that would have been dismissed as fantasy three years earlier. In Japan and South Korea, legacy robotics firms are pivoting toward humanoid form factors. In Europe, research programs are accelerating toward commercialization.

The stated production ambitions vary, but the direction is consistent: humanoid robots manufactured at automotive scale, at automotive prices. Not prototypes for demonstrations. Production models designed for real work in real environments. Multiple companies have announced targets that, even if they miss by a year or two, represent a fundamental shift from laboratory curiosity to commercial product.

When multiple well-funded organizations pursue the same goal simultaneously, the probability that at least one succeeds rises dramatically. And once one demonstrates commercial viability, competitive pressure forces the others to follow. This is not a bet on any single company's timeline. It's a bet on the economics of convergence. And that bet has a strong track record.

The projected price points matter enormously. Several companies have indicated targets in the range of $20,000 to

$50,000 per unit, roughly the cost of a mid-range vehicle. At those prices, a humanoid robot becomes a capital expenditure comparable to a piece of equipment, not a research investment. A small business owner, a warehouse operator, a hospital administrator, these are people who think in terms of equipment budgets, and humanoid robots are entering that range.

Whether the first mass-produced units ship in 2027, 2028, or 2029 is less important than the direction. The humanoid moment is arriving.

Humanoid Form Actually Matters

Critics have questioned whether humanoid form is necessary. Respected robotics researchers have called the vision of humanoid robots as general-purpose assistants unrealistic, noting that robots remain coordination-challenged and that specialized machines outperform generalists at almost every specific task.

They're not entirely wrong about the coordination challenges. But they may be underestimating the economic logic of a humanoid platform.

Consider a warehouse. If you design specialized robots for that warehouse, one type to lift pallets, another to sort packages, another to move inventory, another to clean floors, you need different machines, different maintenance protocols, different training programs, different spare parts inventories.

But if you have a humanoid robot that can walk, grasp objects with dexterous hands, use existing tools, and navigate human spaces, you can deploy the same robot model across multiple tasks. It can sort packages in the morning, clean in the afternoon, and handle inventory restocking at night. The software can be updated, tasks can be changed, but the hardware platform remains constant.

That's the economic advantage of humanoid form. Not that humanoid is optimal for any single task. Specialized machines will often perform better at individual jobs. But humanoid is adaptable across many tasks in environments already built for humans.

And adaptability scales. As the AI improves, the same robot body becomes capable of more complex tasks without hardware changes.

The Hand Problem

For robotics engineers, hands have always been the nightmare. Human hands are extraordinary: 27 bones, 34 muscles, capable of both power grip and precision grip, with tactile feedback so sensitive you can feel a single hair.

Early robot hands were either powerful but clumsy (industrial grippers) or precise but fragile (research prototypes). Getting both strength and delicacy in the same system proved extraordinarily difficult.

Modern humanoid robot hands represent genuine progress: 20-plus degrees of freedom, tactile sensing across palm and fingertips, and AI-driven motor control that can adjust grip pressure in real time. At demonstrations, these robots have handled fragile objects without crushing them, used tools designed for humans, and performed movements that look increasingly natural.

This matters because hands are the interface between thinking and doing. A robot that can think but can't manipulate objects effectively is just an expensive computer. A robot that can both think and physically interact with the world becomes economically viable for real work.

Humanoids Aren't the Whole Story

Humanoid robots make headlines and capture imagination. But the Robot Moment is actually bigger and broader than any single form factor.

The robots transforming society won't all look like humans. Many will be specialized machines that quietly replace labor without resembling people at all. They'll be the unglamorous workhorses that make everything cheaper.

A robot doesn't need to resemble a human to replace a human. It needs to perform a task reliably at a lower cost. That's the real threshold. And once that threshold is crossed, adoption becomes inevitable.

The Five Fronts of the Robot Revolution

Robotics will scale first where the economics are strongest. Not where it's most dramatic or most visible, but where it's most profitable. Here's where the transformation is already underway:

1. Warehouses and Logistics. Warehouses are the hidden cities of modern capitalism, the places where the economy is physically organized. And they're where robots already dominate.

Not humanoids, at least not yet. Specialized machines: autonomous mobile robots that transport goods, sorting systems that process thousands of packages per hour, picking arms that identify and grasp items, inventory-scanning drones that fly through aisles overnight.

The major logistics companies have deployed hundreds of thousands of robots across their operations over the past several years. A large fulfillment center a decade ago might have employed over a thousand people. A comparable facility today handles more volume with significantly fewer workers. The people who remain are more specialized: maintaining robots, handling exceptions, managing the system. But the raw headcount has dropped substantially.

And every improvement compounds. Every efficiency gain means fewer workers needed per million items shipped. The warehouse becomes a choreography of machines with humans in supervisory roles.

2. Manufacturing. Manufacturing has used robots for decades, but modern AI makes them fundamentally more flexible. Old factory robots required extensive reprogramming to handle new products. New factory robots can be retrained with visual examples and adapt to variations.

This makes small-batch production economical, something that was previously impossible without human workers. Factories become less dependent on human labor, achieving more output per worker, more automation per square foot.

Crucially, factories can now be viable closer to consumers because labor is no longer the primary cost driver. When robots do the work, location matters less. Shipping costs start to outweigh labor arbitrage. This has profound implications for global trade, which we'll explore in later chapters.

3. Transportation. This is the front that becomes socially explosive. Because transportation isn't hidden behind warehouse doors. It's visible. And it's one of the largest job categories on Earth.

In the United States alone, millions of people work as truck drivers. Add delivery drivers, taxi and rideshare drivers, bus drivers, and related logistics roles, and you're looking at well over five million jobs directly tied to driving. Globally, tens of millions of people depend on driving for their livelihoods.

Autonomous trucks will likely arrive first on highways. Long-haul routes where the environment is controlled and the economics are compelling. A human driver can legally work about 11 hours per day. An autonomous truck can operate around the clock. That's not just efficiency. It's a fundamental restructuring of logistics economics.

Unlike warehouse automation that happens behind closed doors, every robotaxi is a statement. Every driverless delivery van is a signal. Transportation automation makes the future undeniable and unavoidable. You can't ignore it when it's driving down your street.

4. Construction. Construction is one of the least automated industries in modern life. It's expensive, slow, labor-intensive, and risky. That's about to change.

Robotics will transform construction through several approaches: modular building systems manufactured in factories, robotic fabrication of components, automated site logistics, and autonomous machinery for excavation, grading, and material handling.

Several companies are already 3D-printing houses, laying down concrete layer by layer following a digital blueprint. The technology isn't faster than traditional construction yet in most cases, but it's getting there. And it requires a fraction of the labor.

When construction becomes automated, housing costs could finally decline, one of the automation era's great potential gifts. But it would also displace millions of construction workers globally, people who've built careers on skilled physical labor.

I think about this every time I check in on the house we're building in Garopaba. It's being built the traditional way, with local crews, human hands, the kind of construction that's been done in southern Brazil for generations. I watch the progress photos and I wonder how many years before a building like ours could be assembled largely by machines. Not as a curiosity. As the cheaper option. I suspect it's fewer years than those crews would guess.

5. Healthcare and Elder Care. This is the most emotionally complex frontier because it involves human vulnerability. But it's also where robotics may be most necessary.

Healthcare is filled with tasks that aren't deeply human: transporting linens, delivering meals, moving equipment, monitoring vital signs, tracking medication adherence, documentation, scheduling. These logistics and routine procedures consume enormous amounts of time that doctors and nurses could spend on actual patient care.

Robotics and AI will increasingly handle these tasks, not to replace doctors and nurses as humans but to remove the friction that consumes their time. Japan is already deploying care robots to help elderly patients move, remind them to take medication, and provide companionship. These robots aren't replacing human caregivers. They're supplementing them in situations where human caregivers are scarce or unaffordable.

As populations age globally, care becomes one of the most expensive needs. Robotics will enter healthcare not because it's ideal, but because the demand is too large and the workforce too limited.

Intelligence Changes Everything

Robots aren't new. Factories have used robots for decades. But those robots lived in controlled worlds. They performed repetitive motions. They worked behind cages. They were powerful, precise, and stupid.

They couldn't adapt. They couldn't navigate complex environments. They couldn't handle the messy unpredictability of the real world. They couldn't do what humans do naturally: pick up objects of different shapes, walk around obstacles, interpret context, respond to unexpected situations, and learn from experience.

For a long time, robotics had a missing ingredient. Not motors. Not sensors. Not mechanical design. The missing ingredient was intelligence.

Artificial intelligence changes everything. Robots stop being purely programmed and start being trained. And training scales in ways programming never could.

Consider robotic grasping: for decades, this was robotics' hardest problem. Traditional approaches tried to solve it through explicit programming, defining every possible object, every possible grip angle, every possible interaction. It didn't work. The real world has infinite variation.

Then machine learning arrived. Instead of programming rules, engineers trained neural networks on millions of examples. The robot learned patterns. Learned which approach angles work for soft objects versus rigid ones. Learned how much force to apply. Learned to adapt when the first attempt failed.

By the early 2020s, robotic grasping success rates had reached the threshold where industrial deployment became viable for random objects in cluttered environments. That's the inflection point.

And here's what makes this fundamentally different from previous waves: this is automation that improves itself. Every robot deployment generates more data. More data improves the models. Better models improve all robots. The feedback loop compounds.

Robots Don't Need to Be Perfect

This is one of the most important misunderstandings about automation. People assume robots must be flawless to replace humans. They don't.

Humans aren't flawless. Humans get tired. Humans get distracted. Humans have bad days. Humans make mistakes.

Robots only need to outperform the average human in enough

contexts. Then adoption accelerates. Not because robots are perfect, but because they're more consistent.

Consider autonomous vehicles. Federal highway safety data consistently shows that human error causes the vast majority of serious crashes. Humans drive drunk, drive drowsy, drive distracted, text while driving, speed, misjudge distances, fail to check blind spots.

An autonomous vehicle doesn't need to be perfect to be safer than that. It just needs to be more consistent than we are.

And critically, unlike humans, autonomous vehicles can learn from every mistake made by every vehicle in the fleet. A human driver who rear-ends someone in the rain doesn't make every other driver on Earth more cautious. A networked autonomous fleet does. They improve continuously, collectively, and without forgetting.

This is why autonomy is inevitable. Not because it's glamorous. Because it's statistically superior. And when insurance companies and regulators see that, adoption becomes rational. And once adoption becomes rational, it becomes unstoppable.

The Psychology of Seeing Robots

The Robot Moment won't only change jobs. It'll change perception.

For most people, AI is invisible. They interact with it through chatbots, search results, content feeds, and software tools. It's abstract. It's easy to dismiss as "just software."

Robots are different. Robots are physical. You can see them. You can hear them. You can watch them do something that used to require a person.

That's when the automation era becomes emotionally real. The first time you step into a taxi and there's no driver, something changes. The first time you watch a delivery vehicle arrive at your door without a human inside, something changes. The first time you see a construction site running with more machines than people, something changes.

Robots make the future undeniable. They make it tangible. They turn the abstract concept of automation into a physical presence in daily life.

And that psychological shift matters, because technology adoption isn't just about capability. It's about acceptance. People need to see the future before they believe it's coming.

This Isn't the End of Work

At this point, it's tempting to see robotics as the end of work. It's not.

Robots won't replace all jobs. Not immediately. Not universally. Not evenly.

There will still be work that requires human judgment, creativity, emotional intelligence, ethical decision-making, trust-building. Work that people simply prefer to have done by humans. Teaching young children. Negotiating complex agreements. Providing therapy. Creating art that reflects the human experience.

But robotics will replace enough tasks to weaken the job ladder. And weakening the job ladder changes everything.

Because modern society is built on ladders. The ladder from education to employment. The ladder from entry-level work to middle class. The ladder from middle class to stability.

When the ladder weakens, society becomes more fragile. Opportunity becomes scarcer. Mobility becomes harder. Hope becomes rarer.

And that fragility is what we explore next: how the workforce doesn't collapse in a dramatic wave, but unravels slowly, one disappeared opportunity at a time, until the pattern becomes undeniable.

The Strongest Case for Optimism

Before we proceed with the disruption analysis, intellectual honesty requires presenting the strongest counterargument to this book's thesis. Not the weak version. The strong version. Here's the case that I might be completely wrong, and automation will create more prosperity and employment than it destroys:

First, history is overwhelmingly on the side of job creation. Every major technological revolution, agricultural, industrial, digital, eliminated jobs and created more. The pattern held for 200 years. Betting against this pattern has made fools of every generation of automation pessimists. The Luddites were wrong. The 1960s automation panic was wrong. Why should this time be different?

Second, we consistently underestimate human adaptability and overestimate technology timelines. Autonomous vehicles were "five years away" in 2014. They're still rolling out gradually in 2026. Full humanoid robot deployment might be 15-20 years away, not 5-10. That's enough time for society to adapt, for new industries to emerge, for education systems to evolve.

Third, we can't predict what jobs will emerge because they'll be jobs we haven't imagined yet. In 1995, "social media manager," "app developer," and "podcast producer" didn't exist. In 2035, there will be roles we can't currently conceive. The economy creates work around new technologies.

Fourth, humans have unique advantages that might prove more durable than we expect. Creativity, emotional intelligence, ethical judgment, trust-building, cultural understanding. These may remain economically valuable longer than this book projects. The "human touch" might command premium pricing in an automated world.

Fifth, political and social resistance might slow adoption significantly. If automation threatens widespread unemployment, democracies will regulate, tax, or restrict automation. The transition might take 50 years instead of 20, giving society time to adjust gradually.

Sixth, the "lump of labor fallacy" might apply. This fallacy assumes there's a fixed amount of work. But history shows work expands to fill employment. We might simply redefine what constitutes valuable work. Caregiving, teaching, art, community-building might become the new economy.

Seventh, marginal cost collapse could create infinite demand expansion. When automation drives costs toward zero, consumption explodes. A $70 chair becomes a $20 chair, and everyone can afford three. When goods cost half as much, people don't just save, they buy more. This happened with every cost revolution. Electricity made lighting cheap, people lit entire homes. Computers made processing cheap, entirely new industries emerged. The economy doesn't shrink. It explodes with new demand.

Eighth, human-centric services could explode. As material goods become abundant, value shifts toward human attention, creativity, care, judgment. The care economy could expand dramatically as a share of GDP. The automation economy splits: a lean automated production sector and a vast human services sector. That's transformation, not collapse.

Ninth, the 200-year pattern has never failed. Every generation feared machines. Every generation was wrong. In 1800, 80% of Americans worked in agriculture. By 2000, 2%. Did 78% become unemployed? No. Factories, offices, services, digital industries absorbed them. The pattern has been remarkably consistent: technology eliminates tasks, creates new categories. Betting against human creativity means betting against economic history.

This is the optimistic case at its strongest. And it's not absurd. It's grounded in historical precedent, human resilience, and economic theory.

I don't believe this case, but I respect it. It could be right. The next chapters explain why I think it's wrong this time, but intellectual honesty requires acknowledging it might not be.

Now let's examine why this time might actually be different.

Chapter 3
Why This Time Is Different

I know what you're thinking.

People have been predicting the end of work for decades. The Luddites smashed textile machines in 1811. Economists warned about automation destroying jobs in the 1960s. Every wave of technology has triggered the same panic. And every time, the doomsayers were wrong.

Automation did eliminate jobs. But it also created new ones. Farmers became factory workers. Factory workers became service workers. The economy adapted. People found new roles. The future arrived, and humanity survived.

So why should this time be different?

It's a fair question. It's maybe the most important question in this entire book. Because if this wave of automation is just another chapter in a long story of technological progress, then the alarmism is misplaced. Society will adapt. New jobs will emerge. We'll look back and laugh at the anxiety.

But if this time really is different, if something fundamental has changed, then we need to take it seriously.

I'll tell you when this question stopped being abstract for me. I started hearing the same story from colleagues across financial services, legal, consulting, insurance. Someone would test an AI system on a task their team had been doing manually. The AI would finish in minutes what used to take days. And then there would be a pause, the same pause in every story, where everyone in the room did the same quiet math about what that meant for headcount.

This chapter is my attempt to explain why I believe this time is different. Not as speculation. As structure. Because the automation era isn't just "more technology." It's a categorical shift in what machines can do.

The Pattern That Worked, Until Now

Let's start by acknowledging what's true: automation has always displaced workers. And society has always adapted.

The Agricultural Revolution automated farming. In 1800, roughly 90% of Americans worked in agriculture. By 1900, it was 40%. By 2000, it was 2%. Tens of millions of jobs vanished.

But those displaced farmers didn't starve. They moved to factories. Industrialization created new jobs: manufacturing, logistics, construction. The economy absorbed them.

Then the Industrial Revolution automated physical labor. Machines replaced human muscle. Assembly lines made workers more productive. Again, jobs were destroyed. But new ones emerged: mechanics, engineers, managers. The economy adapted.

Then the Digital Revolution automated routine cognitive work. Computers eliminated typists, switchboard operators, calculators (yes, that was a job). Spreadsheets replaced rooms full of accountants. ATMs reduced bank tellers. But the economy created new roles: programmers, analysts, designers.

Each wave followed the same pattern: technology automated specific tasks, jobs in that sector declined, but productivity increased, which created wealth, which created demand for new goods and services, which created new jobs. Workers transitioned, often over decades.

This pattern held for 200 years. It's why economists developed confidence that technological unemployment is always temporary. It's why the standard response to automation anxiety is: "Don't worry, new jobs will emerge."

And that response has been correct. Until now.

Difference #1: The Speed Is Exponential

The first critical difference is speed. Previous automation waves took generations. This one is taking years.

The Agricultural Revolution took 150 years to fully transform the workforce. People born as farmers died as farmers. Their children might work in factories. The transition was slow enough that society could adapt gradually.

The Industrial Revolution took about 100 years. Again, slow

enough for cultural adaptation, education systems to evolve, and cities to be built.

The Digital Revolution took maybe 40 years. Computers appeared in offices in the 1980s. By the 2020s, they'd reshaped white-collar work. Faster than previous waves, but still decades.

The AI and Robotics Revolution? It's compressing into 15–20 years. Maybe less.

Consider the pace. The first large language models capable of coherent text generation appeared around 2020. By 2023, their successors were passing professional licensing exams, including the bar exam, with scores that placed them above most human test-takers. By 2024, AI coding assistants were being used daily by millions of software developers. That's roughly four years from "interesting toy" to "professional tool."

The trajectory in robotics is similar. The first serious humanoid robot announcements from major companies came around 2021 and 2022. By 2024, multiple platforms were demonstrating complex manipulation tasks in real-world environments. By early 2026, several had moved into early commercial deployment. Five years from concept to production intent.

This speed matters because human institutions can't adapt this fast. Education systems take decades to redesign. Social safety nets take years to build political consensus. Cultural norms about work and identity take generations to shift.

When automation takes 100 years, society can adapt. When it takes 15 years, society gets disrupted.

Difference #2: It's General, Not Specific

The second critical difference is scope. Previous automation was narrow. This automation is general.

Here's what I mean:

The cotton gin automated one specific task: separating cotton fibers from seeds. It didn't pick cotton. It didn't plant cotton. It didn't weave cotton into cloth. Just one task.

The assembly line automated repetitive manufacturing. But it was designed for specific products. A car assembly line couldn't make refrigerators. A shoe factory couldn't make furniture. Each automation was task-specific.

Computers automated calculation and data processing. But early computers couldn't write. They couldn't reason. They couldn't create. They did exactly what they were programmed to do, nothing more.

The AI era is different because it's automating general capabilities: language understanding and generation, visual recognition and interpretation, reasoning and problem-solving, physical manipulation through robotics. Not one task. The underlying abilities that make humans economically useful across thousands of tasks.

When you automate a specific task, workers move to different tasks. When you automate general human capabilities, there's nowhere to move.

A radiologist who spent years learning to read X-rays can't easily transition when AI reads X-rays better. A lawyer who spent a decade mastering legal research can't easily pivot when AI does legal research faster. A programmer who learned to code finds AI generating code from plain English descriptions.

This isn't "some tasks automated, workers do other tasks." This is "the fundamental cognitive and physical capabilities that make humans economically valuable are being automated."

When AI Reads Faster Than Associates

Let me show you what this looks like in practice.

In competitive evaluations conducted over the past several years, AI legal review systems have consistently outperformed experienced human lawyers on standard contract analysis tasks. In one widely cited study, experienced attorneys took over an hour to review a set of contracts and achieved accuracy in the mid-80s percentage range. The AI system completed the same review in under a minute with accuracy in the low-to-mid 90s.

This wasn't a laboratory experiment. By 2024, AI legal review tools had become standard infrastructure at major law firms. Multiple AI legal startups had raised hundreds of millions of dollars in venture capital, not as speculative bets but as validation of products already generating revenue from law firms worldwide.

The impact on hiring is visible. Law firms that once brought in large entering classes of associates have been steadily reducing those numbers. The work that used to fill a junior associate's first two years, contract review, clause flagging, deposition summaries, legal research, is increasingly handled by AI in hours rather than weeks.

The firms still need senior lawyers for strategy, client relationships, courtroom work, and complex judgment calls. But the pathway from law school to senior partner has a missing rung.

I've watched a version of this same pattern at Circle. Tasks in financial compliance, regulatory analysis, and transaction monitoring that once required teams of analysts are increasingly handled by AI systems that work faster, miss less, and don't take weekends. The people who remain in those roles are more senior, more judgment-oriented, more valuable individually. But there are fewer of them. And the entry-level positions that would have trained their replacements are thinning.

Across the legal profession, accounting, consulting, financial analysis, and research, the pattern is consistent: AI is not replacing the senior experts. It is eroding the junior roles that create senior experts. And once those rungs are gone, the entire profession becomes more fragile over time.

Difference #3: There's No Higher Rung

The third critical difference: previous automation waves had escape routes. This one doesn't.

When farming automated, people moved up to factory work. When factories automated, people moved up to service work. When routine service work automated, people moved up to knowledge work.

There was always a "higher rung" on the economic ladder: work that required more skill, more judgment, more creativity. Work that machines couldn't do. Yet.

But what happens when AI can do knowledge work? When robots can do physical work requiring dexterity? When machines have both cognition and physical capability?

There's no higher rung. The ladder ends.

Consider a concrete example. In 2010, if you were a truck driver worried about automation, the advice was: "Learn a skilled trade. Become an electrician or plumber. Those require human judgment and dexterity."

Reasonable advice at the time. But by the mid-2020s, autonomous trucks are in commercial testing, AI systems can diagnose electrical problems from descriptions and images, and humanoid robots are learning to manipulate tools and materials. The "safe" jobs are shrinking. Not slowly. Rapidly. Even skilled trades are in the automation crosshairs within 10–15 years.

The previous pattern was: "Automate low-skill work, humans move to high-skill work." The new pattern is: "Automate everything. Humans... what?"

Difference #4: AI Learns Faster Than Humans

The fourth critical difference is the learning curve.

When a human learns a skill, it takes time. Years to become a doctor. Years to become a lawyer. Years to become a skilled tradesperson. And that knowledge stays in one person's brain.

If you want ten doctors, you need to train ten people for ten years each.

AI doesn't work that way.

When one AI system learns something, that knowledge can be instantly copied to millions of instances. When a language model learns to write code, every copy of that model can write code. When a protein-folding AI learns to predict molecular structures, that capability becomes universally available.

This creates a step-function change, not a gradual transition. One day, AI can't do a particular task. A lab achieves a breakthrough. The next day, every AI system in the world can do that task. The gap between "can't" and "can, at global scale" collapses to nearly zero.

Humans can't compete with that adoption speed. If it takes five years to train a radiologist, but one day for AI to learn radiology and scale to millions of instances, the radiologists can't adapt fast enough.

This is why the "just retrain" advice doesn't work. Retraining takes years. AI capabilities advance in months. The gap is unbridgeable.

Difference #5: The Economic Logic Has Flipped

The fifth critical difference is economic logic.

Previous automation created new jobs because automation created wealth, and wealth created demand.

Here's how it worked: factories automated production. Goods became cheaper. More people could afford goods. Demand increased. Companies needed more workers to meet demand. Employment grew.

This is the classic automation virtuous cycle: efficiency leads to lower prices, which leads to higher demand, which leads to more jobs.

But this logic depends on one assumption: that meeting increased demand requires more human labor.

That assumption is breaking.

If AI and robots can meet increased demand without hiring more humans, the cycle breaks. Production increases. Demand increases. But employment doesn't.

You can see this pattern already in the technology sector. Over the past decade, the largest technology companies have grown their revenues by hundreds of percent while growing their workforces by far smaller proportions. A company can double or triple its output with only a modest increase in headcount, because the growth is absorbed by automation, not by hiring. Revenue scales. Employment doesn't.

Project that forward. What happens when warehouses are 90% robotic? When delivery is autonomous? When customer service is AI? Revenue could double again while employment stays flat, or shrinks.

This is the new economic logic: growth without job creation. Wealth without wage distribution. Abundance without employment.

Previous automation increased productivity per worker. This automation replaces workers entirely.

Addressing the Skeptic

I can hear the objections. Let me address them directly.

"We can't predict what jobs will emerge." True. In 1900, no one predicted "social media manager" or "app developer." New jobs will emerge that we can't imagine. But here's the problem: if AI has general intelligence and robots have general dexterity, they can do the new jobs too. A human might invent a new role, AI ethics consultant, but AI can also do AI ethics consulting. There's no structural reason the new jobs will require humans.

"Humans have creativity and judgment that machines lack." This was true five years ago. It's less true today. And it may not be true in five more years. AI now writes creative fiction, generates art, composes music, designs products. These systems aren't "creative" in a human sense, but economically, that doesn't matter. If an AI can generate a marketing campaign that works, companies will use it instead of hiring human creatives. Judgment is similar. AI legal systems can analyze thousands of precedents and predict case outcomes with accuracy matching or exceeding specialists. "Humans are special" is a nice sentiment. But economically, we're competing. And we're losing ground.

"People said this in the 1960s and were wrong." Yes. And they were wrong because the technology wasn't ready. Computers in the 1960s couldn't reason, couldn't see, couldn't manipulate objects. They were powerful calculators, nothing more. But the technology is ready now. Large language models can reason through complex problems. Computer vision can identify objects with superhuman accuracy. Humanoid robots can manipulate tools. The capabilities that were science fiction in 1964 are engineering reality today. Being wrong in 1964 doesn't mean we're wrong now. It means the technology has finally caught up to the prediction.

What Makes This Time Real

Here's what convinces me this time is genuinely different:

First, the convergence is happening. Advanced language models, computer vision systems, and humanoid robotics are all advancing simultaneously. Each on its own would be significant. Together, they constitute general-purpose automation: machines that can think, see, and physically act in the world. That combination has never existed before.

Second, the economics are working. Companies are already deploying these systems at scale. Not as experiments. As cost savings. Commercial robotaxi services operate in multiple cities. Hundreds of thousands of warehouse robots work alongside (and increasingly instead of) humans in fulfillment centers. AI coding assistants are used daily by millions of developers. When the economics work, adoption accelerates.

Third, the capability curve is exponential. In 2020, the best AI language models couldn't pass a basic high school test. By 2023, the next generation scored in the top percentiles on professional licensing exams, including the bar exam. That's three years from "interesting toy" to "outperforming most professionals." If this curve continues, and it shows no signs of slowing, the implications over the next three to five years are staggering.

The Uncomfortable Truth

I don't enjoy arguing that "this time is different." It sounds arrogant. It invites skepticism. It's the claim every doomsayer makes.

But sometimes, things genuinely are different. Sometimes, the skeptics are wrong. Sometimes, the pattern breaks.

The automation era is different because it's happening in years, not generations. Because it's automating general capabilities, not specific tasks. Because there's no "higher rung" left to climb. Because AI learns and scales faster than humans can adapt. And because economic growth no longer requires employment growth.

This doesn't mean catastrophe. But it does mean we can't rely on historical patterns to guide us. The old rules don't apply.

The question isn't "Will new jobs emerge?" The question is "Will new jobs emerge that humans can do better than AI and robots, and will those jobs emerge fast enough?"

I'm not certain of the answer. But I'm certain the question is different than it was in 1811, 1964, or even 2010.

And that difference, that structural shift in what's possible, is why we need to take this seriously.

What Would Make Me Wrong

I've spent this chapter arguing that automation is different this time. But I could be wrong. And intellectual honesty requires acknowledging what would prove my thesis incorrect.

Here are the specific developments that would invalidate my analysis:

AI progress plateaus. If AI capabilities stop improving significantly by 2030, if the next generation of models delivers only incremental gains rather than transformative leaps, then the automation wave may stall. Current AI might be a local maximum, not the beginning of exponential progress.

New job categories emerge faster than automation. If the economy creates high-quality jobs faster than automation eliminates them, and those jobs are immune to automation for structural reasons I haven't foreseen, then the labor market may remain stable. Perhaps entirely new economic sectors emerge that require uniquely human capabilities.

Robotics remains too difficult. If physical robots can't reliably perform general manipulation tasks by the early 2030s, if dexterity, reliability, and cost remain prohibitive, then automation stays confined to digital work and narrow physical tasks. Manufacturing, logistics, construction, and service work might remain human-dominated much longer than I project.

Political response slows adoption. If societies implement strong regulations limiting automation adoption, requiring human workers for certain tasks, taxing robots heavily, or restricting AI deployment, the economic transition could be much slower. This wouldn't mean the technology doesn't work, but it could mean adoption takes 50 years instead of 20.

Energy costs rise dramatically. The automation economy requires abundant, cheap energy. If energy costs spike due to geopolitical disruption, failed energy transition, or unforeseen constraints, automation becomes less economically viable. Datacenters running AI and factories running robots are energy-intensive. If electricity costs triple, the economics change.

The retraining solution actually works. If I'm underestimating human adaptability and retraining programs prove far more effective than historical precedent suggests, displaced workers might successfully transition at scale. Perhaps AI tutors, online education, and new credential systems enable rapid reskilling that absorbs displaced workers faster than I expect.

New distribution models arrive before the crisis. If universal basic income, social dividends, or entirely new distribution systems get implemented quickly and successfully before major disruption occurs, then the "jobs crisis" never materializes because society has already adapted. Perhaps the political system proves far more responsive than I expect.

These aren't exhaustive, but they're the major scenarios that would invalidate my core thesis. I've tried to make them specific and falsifiable.

The honest truth is that forecasting is hard. Variables interact in unpredictable ways. Black swan events occur. And human systems are more complex than any model.

What I'm confident about: the technology is advancing rapidly, the economic incentives are strong, and the trajectory points toward significant workforce disruption.

What I'm uncertain about: exact timelines, society's response, and whether countervailing forces emerge that I haven't foreseen.

If by 2030–2035 the observable trends suggest I was wrong, I'll be the first to acknowledge it. And honestly, I hope I am wrong, because the alternative is turbulent.

But hope is not a strategy. Which is why we need to prepare for what seems likely, even while acknowledging uncertainty.

Now that we've established why this wave is fundamentally different, and what would prove that analysis wrong, we need to look at what it actually does to the workforce. Not in theory, but in practice.

That's what we explore next.

Chapter 4
The Workforce Unraveling

Robots are easy to understand. A machine replaces a task. A warehouse hires fewer workers. A factory runs with fewer shifts. The cause and effect are visible.

The workforce unraveling is different. It's not a single event. It's not one dramatic wave of layoffs. It's a slow structural shift that feels like a series of unrelated disappointments.

A job search that takes six months longer than it should. A promotion that never materializes. A salary that hasn't budged in five years. An industry that feels colder than it used to. A career that feels less stable than your parents' generation experienced. A college graduate who did everything "right" and still can't find the first rung.

The workforce unraveling doesn't arrive like a tsunami. It arrives like a tide that just keeps coming in.

And the most unsettling part? For a long time, it feels personal.

You blame yourself. You assume you're unlucky. You assume the market is temporary. You assume things will go back to normal. And then, slowly, something becomes clear: this isn't bad luck. This is the economy evolving.

The Ladder Problem

Let me introduce a concept that will help explain why the automation era is fundamentally different from previous transitions. I call it the Ladder Problem.

Modern society is built on ladders: economic pathways that move people from education to employment to stability to prosperity. The education ladder takes you from high school through college to credentials and opportunity. The employment ladder takes you from entry-level work through experience and promotion to security. The skills ladder moves you from manual work through skilled trades to professional expertise. The economic ladder carries you from working class through the middle class toward stability and wealth.

These ladders aren't just metaphors. They're the actual structure that transforms potential into security. And they all share one feature: they require bottom rungs.

The Ladder Problem is this: automation attacks the bottom rungs first, because entry-level work is most automatable. But when you remove the bottom rungs, the entire ladder becomes unclimbable. It doesn't matter how many opportunities exist at the top if no one can reach them.

Consider the traditional path to becoming a senior lawyer: law school, then junior associate doing document review and research, then mid-level associate handling depositions and client work, then senior associate, then partner.

AI now handles document review and much of legal research. The junior associate position, the bottom rung, is shrinking. Firms hire fewer entry-level lawyers. But they still need senior lawyers for strategy and courtroom work. The top rungs remain, but fewer people can reach them.

This creates a paradox: opportunity and scarcity simultaneously. There are still jobs at the top. But the pathway to reach them is broken.

The Ladder Problem appears across professions. In medicine, routine diagnostic work is increasingly handled by AI, reducing the volume of cases that once trained residents. In accounting, AI-assisted bookkeeping and tax preparation thin out the junior roles that once absorbed new graduates. In journalism, automated content generation displaces the entry-level reporting positions where young writers learned their craft. In skilled trades, task-specific robots are beginning to handle work that once required apprentices.

Previous automation waves created new ladders as fast as old ones weakened. Farmers couldn't become factory workers overnight, but their children could. The ladders existed.

The automation era is different because AI and robots can climb the new ladders as fast as humans create them. When a new job category emerges, automation can quickly handle entry-level versions. The Ladder Problem persists.

This isn't about intelligence or capability. It's about structure. When the bottom rungs disappear faster than new ones appear, social mobility collapses. Opportunity becomes hereditary. Those already on the ladder stay; those starting out can't begin.

The Ladder Problem is why the automation era isn't just about unemployment. It's about the collapse of the economic pathways that created the middle class.

Understanding this problem is essential to designing solutions. Because if the problem is broken ladders, the solution isn't retraining (that just tells people to find a different broken ladder). The solution is redesigning how society distributes opportunity when traditional ladders no longer function.

The Ladder Problem is the hidden reason a society can look prosperous on paper while people feel their future has been quietly canceled.

A Story From Right Now

Let me tell you about someone I'll call Rachel, a marketing coordinator in her late twenties. She graduated with good grades from a solid state university, took on $45,000 in student debt, and landed an entry-level position at a mid-sized tech company in 2021.

For four years, she performed well. She managed social media campaigns, coordinated with vendors, analyzed performance metrics, created content calendars. Her reviews were consistently positive. Her work was solid. She was doing exactly what she was supposed to do.

In early 2025, she applied for a promotion to marketing manager, the natural next step on the ladder she'd been climbing. The position had been posted. Her manager had encouraged her to apply. She felt ready.

Two weeks later, the role was eliminated. The company had adopted an AI platform that could generate social content, schedule posts across multiple channels, analyze engagement data in real time, produce performance reports, and even A/B test messaging variations. Tasks that had consumed most of Rachel's time could now be handled by software that cost less than her annual salary.

Her manager assured her it wasn't personal. They still valued her work. They weren't letting her go. But the role she'd been climbing toward no longer existed. The ladder had lost a rung.

She started looking for new opportunities. The market felt different than when she'd started in 2021. Fewer openings. More applicants per position. Job descriptions requiring more skills for the same salary she'd made four years ago. Companies wanting five years of experience for roles that used to require two.

She's not unemployed. She's underemployed. And she's competing with people who have more experience: senior people displaced from higher roles by the same forces that eliminated her promotion path.

This is what unraveling feels like. Not catastrophe. Erosion.

When the First Rung Disappears

Every society has an invisible structure that determines who rises. It's not only intelligence. It's not only hard work. It's not only privilege, though that certainly matters.

It's ladders.

Ladders are the pathways that turn potential into stability. In modern economies, the most important ladder has always been the job ladder: entry-level work, then experience, then skills, then promotion, then stability.

The automation era attacks the first rung. And it's doing it right now.

Entry-level jobs tend to be repetitive, procedural, measurable, standardized, and easy to supervise. In other words: perfect for automation. These aren't the complex judgment calls that require years of experience. They're the routine tasks that teach you the basics while you contribute productive work.

Consider data entry, once a reliable entry point into corporate life. Millions of people built early careers transcribing documents, inputting customer information, processing forms. The work was repetitive but provided steady income and benefits. It was a first rung.

Today, optical character recognition and automated form processing have eliminated most of these roles. Federal labor projections show the occupation declining sharply through the end of this decade. Not because companies don't need the work done, but because software does it faster and cheaper.

The same pattern repeats everywhere. Bank teller positions declining as mobile banking expands. Retail cashier roles shrinking as self-checkout proliferates. Administrative assistant positions consolidating as scheduling and communication tools automate routine tasks. Paralegal positions thinning as AI document review becomes standard.

These weren't glamorous jobs. But they were pathways. Ways for people with high school diplomas or associate degrees to enter stable employment, gain experience, build skills, and climb.

And once the first rung disappears, something dangerous happens. A generation of young people begins to experience adulthood not as opportunity but as rejection.

The Junior Role Problem

Here's a question that should worry us: if junior roles disappear, where do future experts come from?

In the industrial era, companies needed junior workers because they needed hands, eyes, bodies to do the work. Junior roles existed not as charity but as economic necessity. And while doing that work, junior employees learned the business.

But if AI and automation can do entry-level work more efficiently, why hire junior people?

Take law firms. Traditionally, first-year associates spent enormous amounts of time on document review, reading through thousands of pages to find relevant information for cases. It was tedious work, but it taught them how legal arguments were constructed, how evidence was assembled, how cases unfolded. It was apprenticeship through labor.

AI tools are now capable of reviewing documents in hours rather than weeks, identifying relevant passages with accuracy that often matches or exceeds junior human reviewers. Law firms still need senior lawyers for strategy and client relations, but the economic pressure to reduce associate classes is significant and growing. Firms that once hired large entering classes are posting smaller ones.

The same compression is happening across professions. In accounting, AI handles routine audits and tax preparation. In architecture, AI generates initial design variations. In journalism, AI drafts basic news reports. In finance, AI performs fundamental analysis.

So, here's the problem: how does a 25-year-old become a 40-year-old expert if the entry pathway no longer exists?

This is one of the most underestimated long-term consequences of automation. Not mass unemployment. The collapse of professional development pathways. Societies that can't train their next generation of experts become dependent on an aging expert class. And when that generation retires, the knowledge gap becomes structural.

The Hollowing Out of the Middle

After the bottom rung weakens, the middle starts thinning.

This is the phase most people notice. Not because it's dramatic, but because it's familiar. The middle class is where society feels stable. Where mortgages exist, family planning makes sense, retirement seems achievable, and optimism feels rational.

When the middle hollows out, society feels tense.

The automation era hollows out the middle because AI replaces standardized decision-making, routine analysis, administrative workflows, and many coordination tasks.

Meanwhile, robotics replaces repetitive physical labor, warehouse work, and manufacturing roles. And autonomy begins replacing drivers, delivery workers, and transport-related jobs.

This doesn't eliminate all middle-class work. It makes middle-class stability more fragile.

Consider middle management. For decades, mid-level managers coordinated teams, consolidated reports, made resource allocation decisions, and served as communication nodes between executives and workers. These roles required experience and judgment, but much of the actual work was coordination and information synthesis, activities AI increasingly handles well.

An AI system can aggregate performance data from dozens of teams, identify bottlenecks, draft reports, and even suggest resource reallocations based on predictive models. It can't replace the human judgment of a good manager, but it can eliminate the need for several layers of middle management whose primary function was information processing.

The workforce polarizes: those who can leverage AI become more valuable. Those displaced by AI become less secure. The economy produces more while hiring less. More output, fewer humans. This becomes the new corporate pattern.

The Productivity Paradox

Here's one of the strangest emotional experiences of the automation era: people will become more productive and feel less secure.

AI tools help workers produce faster. Write more. Analyze more. Create more. Coordinate more. In many jobs, AI feels like a superpower. And yet, job security weakens.

Because the productivity gain doesn't only benefit the worker. It benefits the employer more. If one person can now do the work of two, the employer needs fewer people.

The worker becomes simultaneously more capable and more replaceable.

This is the paradox. And it's psychologically brutal.

For most of modern history, productivity was rewarded. If you were better at your job, you were safer. You got promoted. You got raises. Being more productive meant being more valuable.

In the automation era, being more productive might simply accelerate the reduction of headcount.

Imagine a graphic designer who adopts AI image generation tools. She can now produce in two hours what used to take her two days. Her output is higher, her creativity is enhanced, her value to the company seems obvious.

But then her company realizes they need fewer designers. The team of twelve becomes a team of five. She's one of the five who remain, for now. But she knows she's producing the work of three people. And she knows that if she leaves or falters, the company might not replace her. They might just redistribute the AI tools to the remaining four.

She's more productive than ever. And more anxious than ever. That's the paradox.

Transportation: The Largest Visible Shock

The workforce unraveling has many fronts. But one will stand out. One will be unavoidable. One will become the symbol of the entire era.

Transportation.

Driving is one of the world's biggest employment categories. Not just in wealthy nations, everywhere. Truck drivers, taxi drivers, bus drivers, delivery drivers, forklift operators, logistics workers.

Transportation has been one of the most reliable ladders into middle-class life. It doesn't require elite credentials. It requires reliability, endurance, skill. And it provides decent income.

Autonomy doesn't augment drivers. It replaces them.

This is why transportation disruption becomes politically explosive. Not because people hate technology, but because they need stability. Because transportation employs too many people. Because it's too visible. Because it's too central to how millions of families make a living.

In the United States, the American Trucking Associations estimates roughly 3.5 million people work as truck drivers. Add delivery drivers, taxi and rideshare drivers, bus drivers, and related logistics roles, and you're looking at well over 5 million jobs directly tied to driving. Globally, the numbers are in the tens of millions.

A warehouse robot can reduce labor quietly, behind closed doors. A self-driving truck is a billboard on the highway. A robotaxi is a public statement every time it pulls up to the curb. A driverless bus is a social shock rolling through residential neighborhoods.

Transportation will make the automation era visible. And once it's visible, the workforce unraveling becomes undeniable.

Consider a long-haul truck driver in his mid-forties. He's been driving for twenty years. He owns his rig, takes pride in his safety record, knows every truck stop between Los Angeles and Chicago. His income is solid. He put his kids through college. He has a mortgage, a retirement plan, a life built around this work.

Now he's seeing autonomous trucks being tested on the highways he drives. He reads articles about companies deploying self-driving freight vehicles. He understands the economics perfectly. He knows that a truck that can drive 24 hours straight without rest breaks is more efficient than he can ever be.

What does he retrain for? At forty-five, with a high school education and two decades of specialized experience that's becoming obsolete? He can't become a software engineer. He can't afford to go back to school for four years. He's too young to retire, too experienced to start completely over easily.

Multiply this story by millions. That's the transportation shock.

The Highway That Runs Itself

Transportation automation isn't theory anymore. It's happening on highways right now.

Multiple companies are operating or testing autonomous freight trucks on commercial corridors across the United States. Some have moved beyond the pilot stage into revenue-generating operations, hauling real freight for paying customers on routes in Texas, Arizona, and other states. The technology is not uniform, the regulatory environment varies by state, and the pace of deployment is uneven. But the direction is unmistakable: driverless commercial trucking is transitioning from research to reality.

The economics explain why. A human long-haul driver works under federal hours-of-service regulations that limit driving time to roughly 11 hours per day. Factor in mandatory rest periods, time off, benefits, and insurance, and the total cost of a human driver runs well into five figures annually. An autonomous system, after the upfront technology investment, can operate nearly around the clock with costs limited to fuel, maintenance, and remote monitoring. The utilization advantage alone is transformative: a truck that runs three times as many hours moves three times as much freight with the same capital equipment.

None of this means human truck drivers disappear next year. Regulatory approval is still uneven. Weather, construction zones, and complex urban environments remain challenging. Labor unions and industry groups are pushing for legislative protections. The transition will take years, possibly decades for full autonomy across all routes and conditions.

But the economic incentive is relentless. And in logistics, where margins are thin and competition is fierce, economic incentives tend to win. The companies that reduce freight costs will capture market share. The companies that don't will lose it. This competitive pressure, not any single company's timeline, is what makes autonomous trucking inevitable.

And unlike warehouse automation, which happens behind closed doors, autonomous trucks are public. Every driverless semi on the highway is a statement. Every autonomous vehicle passing a human driver is a signal. Transportation automation makes the future undeniable.

The highway is already beginning to run itself. The question isn't whether this happens. The question is how society responds when it does.

The Myth of Automatic Replacement

Whenever automation threatens jobs, well-meaning people offer reassurance: "New jobs will appear." "People will retrain." "The economy always adapts."

Historically, that's been true. But history doesn't guarantee the future.

The key question isn't whether new jobs exist. The key questions are: will they appear at the scale needed to replace the old ones? Will they pay comparably? And will they be accessible to average people who've spent decades building expertise in fields that are now automating?

A society can't retrain everyone quickly enough. This isn't pessimism. It's math.

The standard advice used to be: "Learn to code." But that solution has two fatal problems.

First, not everyone is wired for technical roles. Not everyone has the aptitude, the time, or the resources. A 45-year-old truck driver with family obligations can't easily spend two years learning programming while paying a mortgage and supporting kids.

Second, and more importantly: coding itself is being automated. AI tools can now generate functional code from natural language descriptions. Junior programming tasks, the very entry-level roles that would absorb displaced workers learning to code, are themselves being automated.

So, the replacement logic becomes unstable. We're telling people to retrain for jobs that are also automating.

The deeper truth is this: the automation era doesn't eliminate all work. It reduces the amount of human labor needed per unit of output. And that's enough to destabilize the entire wage system.

Work as Identity

Now we arrive at the deeper layer. Work isn't only economic. Work is identity.

In most societies, the first question when meeting someone is: "What do you do?" Not "Who are you?" Not "What do you love?" Not "What do you believe?" What do you do?

That question isn't innocent. It's a social placement test. It locates you in the hierarchy. It determines respect, status, belonging. Work has become a primary identity engine in modern society.

When employment becomes less universal, identity becomes unstable. And when identity becomes unstable, culture becomes unstable.

This is why workforce disruption isn't only about jobs. It's about meaning. Dignity. Status. Belonging.

Studies on long-term unemployment consistently show that the psychological damage goes far beyond financial stress. People report feeling worthless, invisible, ashamed. Their sense of purpose erodes. Their social networks weaken, partly because many friendships are built around work, partly because unemployment carries stigma.

The automation era won't create mass unemployment overnight. But it will create mass underemployment, precarity, and the nagging sense for millions that they're becoming less necessary. That psychological burden is profound.

What It Will Feel Like

The workforce unraveling won't feel like the Great Depression. It won't feel like mass unemployment overnight. It'll feel like something more subtle and more persistent.

A constant sense that the system is tightening. That competition is rising. That wages are stagnant. That companies are less loyal. That careers are less stable. That young people are struggling to begin. That older workers are afraid to lose their foothold. That everything is moving faster. That the world is becoming less forgiving.

This is the emotional landscape of the early automation era. And it shapes politics.

Because politics isn't driven by statistics. It's driven by feeling.

If millions of people feel squeezed, the system destabilizes. Even if GDP rises. Even if stock markets soar. Even if productivity increases. Because humans don't live inside GDP. They live inside rent, groceries, healthcare, and hope.

When enough people feel like the system has stopped working for them, they support disruption. They vote for change, any change. They become susceptible to simplistic narratives that promise to restore what was lost. They become less tolerant, less trusting, less patient.

The New Divide: Secure vs. Insecure

As the workforce unravels, society divides into two groups. Not rich and poor, exactly. Secure and insecure.

The secure class has assets, skills that leverage AI, roles that remain valuable, and the ability to adapt. They own property. They have investment portfolios. They can afford to retrain. They have networks and options.

The insecure class has wages, jobs tied to labor, and limited buffers. They rent. They live paycheck to paycheck. They can't afford to take time off to retrain. They have fewer options when their industry automates.

This division is dangerous because it creates different realities. Different narratives. Different politics.

One group experiences the automation era as opportunity: tools that amplify their capabilities, technologies that make life more convenient, an economy that rewards their adaptability.

The other experiences it as betrayal: a system that no longer needs them, technologies that threaten their livelihoods, an economy that leaves them behind.

And both are telling the truth from their perspective.

This is why the automation era will be politically turbulent. Not because technology is evil. Because transitions create winners and losers. And the losers don't disappear quietly.

The Distribution Problem Emerges

The workforce unraveling isn't the final crisis. It's the beginning.

Because once enough jobs weaken, once enough people feel economically insecure, once the connection between productivity and employment breaks down sufficiently, society faces the most unavoidable question of the automation era:

If machines produce the wealth, how do humans receive income?

This is the distribution problem. And it's where economics becomes politics. Where politics becomes culture. Where technical questions become existential ones.

When Does This Actually Happen?

Before we go further, you need a timeline. Because "the automation era" sounds abstract. Let me make it concrete.

The transformation happens in waves, not all at once. Here's the gradient:

Phase 1: Augmentation and Early Disruption (2024–2029).
AI tools become standard in knowledge work: legal research, code generation, document review, marketing content, customer service. These don't eliminate jobs immediately. They reduce headcount growth and eliminate junior positions. Warehouse robotics expand significantly. Major logistics companies deploy hundreds of thousands of robots. Human warehouse employment stops growing despite rising package volumes. Autonomous trucks begin commercial operations on major freight corridors. Not everywhere, but enough to be visible. Long-haul trucking jobs start declining in specific regions.

Phase 2: Major Displacement (2029–2035). AI capabilities expand dramatically. Tasks that seemed "safe" in 2025, creative work, complex analysis, specialized knowledge, become partially automated. The junior-to-mid-career ladder breaks across multiple professions. Humanoid robots or specialized automation systems become economically viable for manufacturing, warehouses, and some service roles. Not universal, but widespread enough to impact millions of workers. Autonomous vehicles expand beyond highways. Urban robotaxis. Autonomous delivery. The transportation workforce begins significant decline.

Phase 3: Structural Labor Compression (2035–2045). The economy produces more than ever with far fewer workers. Not because of recession, but because of automation. Labor force participation declines not from choice but from scarcity of available work. Distribution systems must redesign. Some form of social income becomes political necessity in multiple countries. The "job ladder" as the default life path weakens dramatically. Purpose, meaning, and identity questions intensify. Culture begins evolving, slowly, to honor contribution beyond employment.

The Key Point

We're in Phase 1 right now. You're reading this book during the early disruption. The massive displacement comes in 5–10 years. The structural redesign comes in 10–20 years.

This isn't "someday." This is a gradient you're already on.

The rest of this book explores what happens at each phase, and what we can do about it.

Now that we've established why this wave is fundamentally different, what would prove that analysis wrong, and when it's happening, we need to look at what it actually does to the workforce. Not in theory, but in practice.

That's what we explore next.

Chapter 5
The Economics of
Labor Going to Zero

The Economic Engine

Let me walk you through the economic logic that drives the entire automation era. Not as theory. As mechanism. This is the engine underneath everything we've discussed so far.

I want to start with something personal, because the abstraction of economics can make a devastating process feel bloodless. Before I worked in technology, I studied finance. I spent years in environments where people thought in terms of cost optimization, margin improvement, headcount efficiency. These are clean phrases. They mean firing people. They mean replacing human judgment with cheaper alternatives. They mean deciding that a process done by twelve people can be done by four people and a software tool, and then making the eight people disappear from a spreadsheet.

I'm not being cynical. This is how businesses work. This is how they've always worked. The difference now is that the cheaper alternative isn't a person in a lower-cost country or a slightly better machine. The cheaper alternative is no person at all.

Understanding this mechanism is crucial because it explains why the automation era is inevitable, why "the market will adjust" doesn't solve it, and why we need entirely new distribution systems.

The engine underneath the automation era is not mysterious. It's incentives compounding. Four steps.

Step 1: Labor Cost Creates the Price Floor

For most of human history, the cost of production had a floor. That floor was labor.

You can make materials cheaper. You can make capital equipment more efficient. You can optimize logistics. But you cannot make human workers free.

A human requires food, shelter, healthcare, and a minimum survival income. In developed economies, this creates a wage floor. Below a certain annual income, people cannot survive. Below that threshold, society becomes unstable. This wage floor propagates through the entire economy as a price floor.

Consider a simple product: a wooden chair. In traditional manufacturing, the cost breaks down roughly into raw materials, capital equipment, labor, and overhead. The exact proportions vary, but in many manufactured goods, labor accounts for somewhere between a third and half of the final price. And that labor cost cannot fall below the survival threshold. The carpenter cannot work for a wage that doesn't cover rent. The market has a biological floor: human survival requirements.

This creates a fundamental coupling in traditional economics: human labor is required, labor cost has a biological floor, and product prices reflect that floor.

Everything in the economy is priced with this floor baked in. Your groceries. Your housing. Your healthcare. Your education. All of it includes the cost of the human labor required to produce it.

This isn't a bad thing. This is how societies distributed purchasing power. Wages were the mechanism. If you wanted to earn income, you sold your labor. The economy needed labor, so labor had value.

But automation breaks this coupling.

Step 2: Automation Collapses Marginal Cost

Now introduce automation. Not partial automation, but the kind we're entering now, where AI and robots can perform an increasing percentage of tasks with minimal human oversight.

Return to the chair. When a robotic assembly system replaces the carpenter, the labor component of that chair's cost doesn't just shrink. It collapses. The robot doesn't need a living wage. It needs electricity and maintenance. The labor cost that might have been a third or more of the chair's price drops to a fraction, perhaps a tenth of what it was.

But here's the crucial insight: this is only the beginning. The first factory to automate might achieve a 50% labor cost reduction. But as the technology improves and scales, labor cost approaches zero asymptotically. Within a few years, the cost of the human work in that chair goes from substantial to negligible to a rounding error. What remains is the cost of materials plus energy.

This is fundamentally different from previous automation waves.

Previous automation made workers more productive. One worker with a power tool could do the work of three workers with hand tools. But you still needed the worker. Labor became more efficient, but it remained essential.

AI and robotics don't make labor more efficient. They make labor optional.

When labor becomes optional, labor cost goes to near-zero. And when labor cost goes to near-zero, prices can fall dramatically.

I saw a version of this logic play out in finance, years before robots entered factories. When electronic trading replaced floor traders, the cost of executing a stock trade dropped from tens of dollars to pennies. The humans on the floor weren't just made more efficient. They were made unnecessary. The exchange floor didn't thin out gradually. It emptied. The same economic logic that emptied the trading floor is now headed for the factory floor, the warehouse floor, the office floor.

Step 3: Scale Creates Abundance

Here's where it gets interesting. Because once production becomes automated, scale becomes cheap.

In a traditional factory, if you want to double output, you hire twice as many workers. Labor cost scales linearly with output. Every additional unit of production requires an additional unit of human effort, and that effort has a biological price floor.

In an automated factory, if you want to double output, you add more machines. Machines are a capital expenditure. You buy them once, then pay marginal operating costs. The difference between 100 workers and 200 workers is millions of dollars per year in ongoing salary. The difference between 100 robots and 200 robots is a one-time capital outlay, followed by modest incremental operating costs for electricity and maintenance.

After the initial capital investment, scaling production becomes dramatically cheaper.

And here's the compounding effect: as production scales, fixed costs get amortized across more units, driving per-unit costs down further. A factory producing ten times as many goods spreads its overhead across ten times as many items. The cost per item drops not just because labor is cheaper, but because every fixed cost in the system, the building, the equipment, the design, the management, gets divided by a larger number.

The same chair that costs a certain amount under human labor might cost a third or a quarter of that at scale with full automation. Not because materials got cheaper. Because the human labor component, which used to be the largest cost driver, has effectively disappeared.

This is the abundance dynamic: automation enables scale,

scale reduces costs, reduced costs enable more consumption, more consumption enables more scale. It's a reinforcing loop.

The economy can produce vastly more goods at vastly lower costs. This is why the book is titled "The Age of Abundance." Because automation doesn't just make production more efficient. It makes scarcity increasingly optional for manufactured goods.

But, and this is crucial, abundance is not the end of the story. It's where the real problem begins.

Step 4: Abundance Collapses Labor Demand

Now we arrive at the paradox. The brutal, unavoidable paradox at the heart of the automation era.

The economy produces abundance. Costs fall. Goods become cheaper. Supply increases. This should be unambiguously good.

But there's a problem: who can afford to buy the abundance?

In the traditional economy, production and distribution were coupled through wages. The factory needed workers. Workers earned wages. Wages created purchasing power. Purchasing power created demand. Demand justified production. It was a closed loop.

Automation breaks the loop. Production continues, but it no longer needs workers. Without workers, there are no wages. Without wages, there is no purchasing power. Without purchasing power, there is no demand.

Let's make this concrete. Imagine a factory that employed a hundred people, each earning a middle-class income. That's millions of dollars in annual wages flowing into the local economy. Those workers spend their wages on housing, food, clothing, entertainment, and yes, furniture. The factory and the community around it exist in a symbiotic loop: the factory needs workers, the workers need the factory, and both need the economy that connects them.

Now automate that factory. It produces ten times as many goods with a fraction of the workforce. Production is up. Cost per unit is down. By every traditional economic measure, this is progress.

But the factory eliminated most of its jobs. Those workers no longer have wages. They no longer create demand. And it's not just this factory. Every factory automates. Every warehouse automates. Every logistics company automates. Millions of workers lose wage income across the economy.

So yes, goods are dramatically cheaper. But if you don't have a job, you can't afford even dramatically cheaper goods.

The economy can produce more than ever. But fewer people can afford to buy what's produced.

This is the abundance paradox: productivity increases, costs fall, supply explodes, but demand collapses because wage income disappears.

I grew up watching a version of this in Brazil, though the mechanism was different. Brazil has always been a country capable of producing enormous wealth. Agriculture, mining, manufacturing, the productive capacity was there. But the distribution was broken. Gated condominiums two blocks from favelas. Supermarkets overflowing with food in cities where children went hungry. Abundance and deprivation, side by side, separated not by scarcity but by a distribution system that couldn't connect production to the people who needed it. The automation era risks creating this same disconnect, not in one country but globally. Not because of corruption or mismanagement, but because the fundamental mechanism that distributed purchasing power, the wage, is breaking.

The Full Economic Engine

Let me show you the complete sequence.

Step 1: Labor creates the price floor. Humans need survival income, so wages have a biological floor, and prices reflect labor cost.

Step 2: Automation collapses marginal cost. Robots don't need survival income. Operating cost approaches the cost of energy. Prices can fall dramatically.

Step 3: Scale creates abundance. Automated production scales cheaply. Fixed costs amortize across more units. Per-unit cost collapses. Supply explodes.

Step 4: Abundance collapses labor demand. Production doesn't need workers. Jobs disappear. Wages disappear. Purchasing power disappears. Demand collapses.

The result: the economy produces more than ever, but fewer people can afford to buy. Distribution crisis.

This is the economic engine of the automation era. It's not a bug. It's the direct, inevitable result of the economic logic.

Why "The Market Will Adjust" Doesn't Work

Now you understand why the standard economic response, "the market will adjust," doesn't solve this.

Yes, prices will fall. That's Step 3. Abundance is real.

But no, demand won't automatically return. Because demand requires purchasing power. And purchasing power, for most people, comes from wages. And wages disappear when labor is automated.

The market can't adjust wages low enough to compete with robots without causing human starvation. And the market can't create new jobs automatically when AI and robots can do the new jobs too.

There's no market-clearing price for labor when labor competes with machines whose annual operating cost is a fraction of a human's annual survival requirement. The machine costs what the electricity costs. The human costs what life costs. That's not a gap the market can close.

The wage system breaks. Not because of policy failure. Because of math.

Why This Requires New Distribution Systems

This is why the automation era forces a redesign of distribution systems.

The old system was straightforward: produce goods, pay wages, workers buy goods, the loop continues.

The new system needs a different middle step. Produce goods, then somehow ensure citizens have purchasing power, then citizens buy goods, and the loop continues.

That "somehow" is the question the automation era forces us to answer.

Maybe it's universal basic income. Maybe it's social dividends. Maybe it's public ownership of automation infrastructure. Maybe it's some hybrid we haven't imagined yet.

But it can't be wages. Because wages require jobs. And jobs are disappearing not because of bad policy but because of economic inevitability.

When robots cost less than humans and perform tasks reliably, companies automate. When companies automate, jobs disappear. When jobs disappear, wages disappear. When wages disappear, demand disappears.

That's the engine. That's the mechanism. That's why we can't just "let the market handle it."

What This Means Going Forward

Everything else in this book builds on this economic engine. The workforce unraveling? That's Step 4 beginning. The distribution crisis? That's Step 4 reaching critical mass. The need for new economic models? That's the response to Step 4. The purpose problem? That's what happens when Step 4 is complete.

Understanding this engine is essential. Because once you see the mechanism clearly, you understand why this isn't temporary. It's structural. Why retraining doesn't solve it. Why wage cuts don't solve it. Why market forces don't solve it. Why we need new distribution systems.

The automation era is the economy becoming productive enough to generate abundance but structurally unable to distribute that abundance through the wage system.

That's the challenge. That's the opportunity. That's why the title of this book is "The Age of Abundance" rather than "The Age of Unemployment."

Because the production problem is solved. The distribution problem is not.

And solving the distribution problem is the defining challenge of the century.

I think about this when I look at the work I do at Circle. Stablecoins, digital payments, programmable money. These are tools that could become part of the distribution infrastructure for the automation era. The technology to move value instantly, cheaply, and globally already exists. The question is whether we'll build the political and economic systems to use it. Whether the pipe that delivers abundance to people will be as well-designed as the machines that produce it.

Now let's look at what this means for specific sectors and specific people. Because economic engines are abstract. Job losses are personal.

Chapter 6
The Psychological Shock

The economics are brutal. But economics are abstract. GDP. Labor force participation. Wage share. Unemployment rates. These are numbers.

The psychological impact is different. It's personal. It's identity. It's self-worth. It's the answer to "Who am I?" And when that answer is stripped away, the human cost becomes something statistics cannot capture.

This is the chapter I almost didn't write. Not because the material is hard to find, but because it's hard to face. I've managed teams through restructurings. I've watched talented people learn that their roles were being eliminated. I've seen the moment it lands, not the anger, that comes later, but the blankness. The instant where someone's internal narrative about who they are and where they're going suddenly has no next page. That blankness is what this chapter is about.

Because the automation era doesn't only redistribute income.

It redistributes meaning. And meaning is harder to replace than money.

The Identity Collapse

For most of modern history, work provided identity.

"What do you do?" is one of the first questions strangers ask. Not "Who are you?" Not "What do you care about?" But "What do you do?" Meaning: what is your job?

The answer carries enormous weight. It signals status, education, capability, ambition, contribution. A surgeon. A teacher. A carpenter. An engineer. A truck driver. Each carries an identity. A story. A place in the world.

Work wasn't only income. It was selfhood.

And when work disappears, identity fractures.

Consider David, 52, a manufacturing supervisor who's worked at the same automotive plant for 28 years. He started on the assembly line at 24, worked his way up to team leader, then supervisor. He's proud of his career. He knows the production floor better than anyone. He's trained dozens of younger workers. He's solved problems, improved processes, kept the line running during crises.

His job is who he is. When people ask what he does, he doesn't just say "I work in manufacturing." He says, "I'm a production supervisor at the plant." It's identity.

Then the plant announces automation. Robotic assembly systems will replace the majority of the line workers over the next 18 months. David's role, supervising humans, becomes obsolete when there are no humans to supervise. The company offers him early retirement at 54 with a decent pension.

Financially, he's fine. The pension covers his expenses. His mortgage is nearly paid off. His kids are grown. He's not facing poverty.

But he's facing something worse: irrelevance.

For 28 years, he was the guy who kept the line running. He was the one people came to with problems. He had expertise, authority, purpose. He knew his role. He knew his value.

Now what is he?

A retiree at 54. A guy who used to work at a plant that doesn't need him anymore. A guy whose skills are obsolete. A guy with no answer when someone asks "What do you do?"

This is identity collapse. And it's psychologically devastating.

The psychological shock intensifies when people realize the Ladder Problem is structural, not personal. That their inability to advance isn't a failure but a missing pathway.

Studies on early retirees and displaced workers show consistent patterns: increased rates of depression, substance abuse, anxiety, and even early mortality. Not because of poverty. Many have adequate income. Because of purposelessness.

Humans are not wired for aimlessness. We need structure. We need contribution. We need identity. When work provided all three, losing work meant losing all three.

The automation era risks creating millions of Davids. Not unemployed in the traditional sense, but unmoored. Financially stable but existentially adrift.

I think about my father when I write this. He's retired now, in Garopaba, and he's one of the lucky ones. He has community, family nearby, a rhythm to his days that doesn't depend on a job title. But I've watched other men in his generation retire and shrink. Men whose entire identity was built around the work, and who discovered that without it, they didn't know who they were. The automation era is going to create that experience at scale, for people decades younger than retirement age, in a society that has no cultural script for it.

The Status Wound

Identity loss is personal. Status loss is social. And humans are intensely, unavoidably social creatures.

We care about status. Not because we're shallow, because we're tribal. For hundreds of thousands of years, status within the tribe meant survival. High-status individuals had access to resources, mates, protection, influence. Low-status individuals were vulnerable.

Modern civilization dressed up status in new clothes, job titles, income levels, educational credentials, professional respect, but the underlying psychology remained. Status matters. And work was one of the primary ways societies allocated status.

The automation era doesn't distribute status loss evenly. It concentrates it.

Some jobs carry high status: doctors, lawyers, executives, engineers, professors. Other jobs carry moderate status: teachers, nurses, skilled tradespeople, managers. And some jobs carry low status but still provide dignity: warehouse workers, drivers, retail workers, service staff.

When automation eliminates jobs, it doesn't just eliminate income. It eliminates status positions. And the people who lose those positions feel the wound socially.

Consider Elena, 38, a legal associate at a mid-sized law firm. She spent three years in law school, passed the bar, took on six figures of debt, and worked brutal hours to build her career. She's not a partner yet, but she's on track. She has a business card. An office. A title. Respect.

Then the firm adopts AI legal research and document review tools. The work that consumed most of her time, analyzing case law, reviewing contracts, summarizing depositions, now takes the AI minutes instead of days.

The firm doesn't fire her. They "restructure." They reduce the associate class significantly. Elena isn't in the group that stays. She's offered a severance package and encouraged to "explore other opportunities."

She finds another position, eventually. But it's at a smaller firm, for less money, with less prestige. She's no longer on a partner track. She's no longer building a prestigious career. She's a contract worker. Disposable. Replaceable. Generic. At social events, when people ask what she does, she feels the shift. The subtle devaluation. The loss of respect.

This is the status wound. And it affects people across the income spectrum.

A truck driver who loses their job to autonomous vehicles doesn't just lose income. They lose the identity of being a professional driver, someone with skills, licenses, expertise. They become "unemployed former driver." The status drops.

A warehouse supervisor replaced by robotic systems doesn't just lose a paycheck. They lose authority, respect, the sense of being needed. They become redundant.

Status wounds don't heal with money alone. You can give someone a basic income to replace lost wages. But you can't give them back the social respect they lost when their profession became obsolete.

And when millions of people experience status loss simultaneously, society becomes resentful, angry, and politically volatile.

Community Disintegration

Work didn't only provide identity and status. It provided community.

For many people, work was where they spent most of their waking hours. Where they had friends. Where they belonged to a team. Where they shared jokes, frustrations, victories, rituals.

The automation era risks dismantling these communities without replacing them.

Consider a factory town. Generations worked at the same plant. People met their spouses there. They coached their kids' soccer teams with their coworkers. They went to the same bars after shifts. They had shared experiences, shared hardships, shared pride in what they built.

Then the factory automates. Employment drops dramatically. The plant is still there, still producing, more than ever. But most of the people who used to come to work no longer do. The rituals disappear. The friendships disperse. The community unravels.

This isn't unique to factories. Office workers lose the daily interactions with colleagues. Drivers lose the camaraderie of truck stops and dispatch centers. Teachers lose the faculty lounge. Retail workers lose the break room bonds.

Remote work already began this shift. Many knowledge workers work from home, connect through video calls, and miss the informal hallway conversations and lunch discussions that built relationships.

The automation era accelerates this. If work becomes less central to life, either because jobs are scarce or because basic income provides stability without employment, where do people find community?

Some will build new communities around hobbies, causes, local organizations, civic engagement. But this requires intention, effort, and social infrastructure that doesn't currently exist at scale.

Many will drift into isolation. Digital connections, social media, online gaming, virtual friendships, provide some interaction but lack the depth and richness of face-to-face community. Loneliness is already an epidemic in developed nations. Rates of social isolation have risen steadily for decades. Participation in civic organizations has declined. Close friendships have thinned. The automation era risks intensifying all of this.

Because community doesn't arise automatically. It requires shared context. Shared purpose. Shared struggle. Work provided all three. When work weakens, community weakens. And humans are not designed for isolation.

This is part of why I'm planning on building a life in Garopaba. Not just a house. A life in a place where community still functions the way communities used to, where people know each other, where meals happen without scheduling apps, where kids play in the street and the neighbors watch them. It's not nostalgia. It's a bet that the places where social fabric is still intact will be the places that handle the automation era best. Because when the economic structures weaken, what holds people together is each other. And that requires proximity, familiarity, and the kind of daily contact that no algorithm can replicate.

Meaning Without Necessity

Here's the deepest psychological challenge: how do humans find meaning when survival doesn't require effort?

For all of human history, meaning was partially answered by necessity. You had to work to survive. You had to contribute to your family, your tribe, your community. There was no choice.

That necessity was often brutal. But it provided structure. It provided purpose. You knew what you had to do. And doing it gave life meaning. Even if that meaning was simply survival.

The automation era weakens this necessity. If basic income provides stability, if robots produce abundance, if survival is decoupled from labor, where does meaning come from?

Some people will thrive. They'll pursue education, art, caregiving, community service, mastery of crafts, exploration of ideas. They'll build lives rich with purpose because they're self-directed, curious, disciplined.

But not everyone is wired this way. And that's not a moral judgment. It's reality. The self-directed entrepreneur and the externally-structured worker are both valid human types. Neither is better. They just face the automation era differently.

For many people, meaning came from external structure. The job gave them a reason to wake up. The boss gave them tasks. The paycheck gave them validation. The career ladder gave them direction.

Remove that structure, and they drift.

We've seen this pattern in early retirees, lottery winners, and trust fund inheritors. Research consistently shows that sudden freedom from work often leads to depression, substance abuse, relationship breakdown, and aimlessness. Not universal, but common enough to be concerning.

Why? Because freedom without purpose is overwhelming.

Viktor Frankl, a psychiatrist and Holocaust survivor, wrote extensively about meaning. He observed that humans can endure almost any hardship if they have a sense of purpose. But they struggle deeply with comfort without purpose.

In concentration camps, those who found meaning, caring for others, maintaining dignity, holding onto hope, survived psychologically. Those who lost meaning often gave up, even when physically capable of surviving.

The automation era risks creating the opposite condition: physical abundance without psychological meaning. Comfort without purpose. Survival without necessity.

This is not a trivial problem. This is the problem.

Because humans don't only need food, shelter, and safety. We need to matter. We need to contribute. We need to feel that our existence serves something beyond ourselves.

When work provided that automatically, the question of meaning was answered, partially, by default. The automation era removes that default answer. And many people will struggle to find a new one.

The Psychological Divide

Not everyone will experience the automation era the same way psychologically.

Some people are self-directed. They have hobbies, passions, projects, relationships that define them independent of work. For them, losing a job is disruptive but not existentially devastating. They'll adapt. They'll find new purpose. They'll thrive.

But others are externally structured. They rely on jobs, bosses, schedules, and social expectations to provide direction. This isn't weakness. For most of human history, external structure was the norm. Self-direction is a recent expectation, and a difficult one.

For them, losing work is identity collapse. They struggle to create their own purpose. They drift.

This creates a psychological divide that mirrors the economic divide.

The wealthy and secure can pursue meaning on their own terms. They have resources, education, networks, time. They become artists, philanthropists, lifelong learners, community builders.

The insecure and struggling face both economic anxiety and existential anxiety. They need income and need purpose. The automation era threatens both.

This divide doesn't only create inequality of wealth. It creates inequality of meaning. And inequality of meaning may be more corrosive to society than inequality of income.

Because a person with money but no purpose is miserable. And a society of miserable people is unstable.

Why This Matters More Than Economics

Economists focus on GDP, employment, income distribution. These matter. But they're incomplete.

The automation era's deepest challenge isn't producing enough wealth. It's distributing meaning.

You can solve the economic problem with universal basic income, social dividends, public ownership of automation infrastructure. These are hard, but they're solvable.

But how do you solve the psychological problem? How do you give people identity when work no longer provides it? How do you give people status in a world where traditional status markers are obsolete? How do you build community when shared work no longer creates it? How do you cultivate meaning when necessity no longer demands it?

These aren't economic questions. They're human questions. And they don't have policy solutions. They have cultural solutions.

Culture must evolve to honor contribution beyond employment. To respect caregiving, mentorship, art, service, learning. To create new rituals, new communities, new sources of belonging.

Education must teach not only skills but also self-direction, meaning-making, purpose cultivation. Schools must prepare young people not only for jobs but for lives where jobs are scarce or optional.

Individuals will need to cultivate internal purpose rather than relying on external validation. This is hard work. Psychologically harder than showing up to a job.

And this difficulty deserves acknowledgment. Disorientation will be normal. Confusion is expected. Feeling lost when the structure disappears isn't a personal failing. It's a predictable human response to having the rules changed.

Purpose cannot be imposed. It must be discovered, built, sometimes painfully rebuilt. Some people will find it quickly. Others will struggle for years. Both experiences are valid. Both deserve support, not judgment.

The automation era asks something unprecedented: that people create meaning in a world that no longer demands their labor for survival. This is psychologically sophisticated work. It requires self-awareness, discipline, resilience, and often support from others.

Expecting everyone to navigate this transition smoothly is unrealistic. Offering compassion and infrastructure to help people through it is essential.

A society of distracted, purposeless citizens is easy to control. But that risk isn't a moral failing of individuals. It's a structural challenge of civilization. The response cannot be "try harder." The response must be systemic support for meaning-making: community organizations, accessible mental health resources, cultural permission to explore purpose beyond employment, and economic stability that allows experimentation without fear.

If you're reading this and feeling anxious about your own ability to find meaning without work, that anxiety is reasonable. This transition will be hard. Harder for some than others, through no fault of their own. The goal isn't to shame anyone for struggling. It's to acknowledge the challenge so we can build support systems that help people through it.

Compassion, not judgment, is what the automation era requires.

The Test of Civilization

The automation era is testing whether human civilization can handle abundance.

Scarcity is brutal, but it's simple. When resources are limited, the challenge is survival. Everyone understands survival. It's primal. It's clear.

Abundance is kind, but it's complex. When resources are plentiful, the challenge is meaning. And meaning is not primal. It's constructed. It's fragile. It requires intention.

I'll be honest: I don't know how my own kids will navigate this. Luca is sixteen and already thinking about what he wants to study, what career he wants to build. The advice I'd give him is fundamentally different from the advice my parents gave me, which was fundamentally different from what their parents told them. My parents said: get a stable job. My generation said: follow your passion but be practical. What do I tell Luca? Build skills that complement AI? Learn to create meaning independent of employment? Both feel inadequate. Both feel true.

Societies that successfully navigate the automation era will be those that recognize this. That understand the economic transformation is secondary to the psychological transformation.

Because an economy that produces abundance but creates aimlessness is not a success. It's a crisis in slow motion.

The next chapters explore how we might redesign distribution systems, education, and social structures to support meaning in the age of abundance. But none of that matters if we don't first understand what we're solving for.

We're not solving for wealth. We're solving for lives worth living.

And that's a much harder problem.

Chapter 7
The Distribution Crisis

The workforce unraveling creates anxiety. But anxiety is still built on an assumption: That the system will correct itself. That jobs will return. That wages will catch up. That the market will adjust. That new industries will appear. That the old model will somehow survive.

The automation era challenges that assumption at its foundation. Because it changes the relationship between production and employment in a way that can't be easily reversed.

And once that relationship changes, the old model of income distribution begins to fail. Not as ideology. As arithmetic.

This might be the most important chapter in the book. Because it's where we stop talking about 'jobs being disrupted' and start confronting something more fundamental:

The wage system stops functioning as the default way society distributes income.

Not overnight. Not universally. But meaningfully enough to force a complete redesign of how modern economies work.

The Deal That Built Modern Civilization

For most of modern history, the economy ran on a simple loop:

People work → wages are paid → people consume → companies grow → companies hire more people.

This loop did more than create prosperity. It created stability, predictability, and the sense that life made sense. You worked. You earned. You built. You retired. Even if the system was unfair, and it often was, it was at least legible. You could understand it. You could plan inside it.

The wage system wasn't just about compensating people for their time. It was the distribution system of modern civilization. It ensured that the majority of citizens could participate in the economy. It was the mechanism that allowed capitalism to function without collapsing into oligarchy.

And it worked, imperfectly, for a long time.

Consider the post-World War II American economy. Between 1945 and 1973, productivity roughly doubled, and median family income roughly doubled as well. The gains from economic growth were broadly shared. When companies became more efficient, they hired more workers. When demand increased, wages rose. The system wasn't perfect, but the basic mechanism functioned: economic growth translated into widespread prosperity.

This era created the modern middle class. It funded the expansion of homeownership, higher education, healthcare systems, and retirement security. It made the American Dream feel achievable for millions.

But something changed around the 1970s. Productivity kept rising, but wages began to flatten. Between 1973 and 2020, productivity increased by roughly 77%, while typical worker compensation rose by only 18%. The loop started breaking.

The automation era doesn't start this pattern, it accelerates it. Because it creates a world where production can rise while wages stagnate. Where the economy can grow while citizens feel poorer. Where companies can expand while hiring less.

When Growth and Jobs Decouple

In the industrial era, productivity and employment were tightly linked. If a company grew, it hired more people. If demand rose, more workers were needed. If output increased, wages tended to rise. Not perfectly. Not always. But broadly.

The automation era severs this link.

A company can grow without hiring. A factory can expand output without adding shifts. A warehouse can process more orders with fewer workers. An office can complete more tasks with a smaller team.

The economy becomes more productive without needing proportionally more humans. This isn't theory, it's happening right now.

Look at the technology sector. Between 2010 and 2020, the combined market value of major tech companies increased by trillions of dollars. But their combined employment grew modestly. Google created enormous value with relatively few employees compared to industrial giants of previous eras. General Motors employed over 600,000 workers at its peak. Google, despite its massive economic impact, employs around 180,000.

Or consider Netflix. The company effectively dismantled the video rental industry, which once employed hundreds of thousands of people at chains like Blockbuster. Netflix delivers more content to more people than Blockbuster ever could, but employs a fraction of the workforce.

The pattern is clear: digital technologies enable companies to scale value without scaling employment proportionally. The automation era extends this from digital services to physical goods and services.

The Hidden Truth About Wages

This is where many discussions get confused. People treat wages as if they're simply compensation for labor. But wages were always more than that.

Wages were the distribution system of modern civilization. They were how the wealth created by the economy reached the population.

In a world where humans do most of the work, wages are a natural distribution mechanism. But in a world where machines do an increasing share of the work, wages become insufficient. Not because employers become evil. Because the system changes.

When a machine replaces a human worker, the company's costs decline. Output rises. Profit increases. But the displaced worker loses income. The wealth created by automation flows to owners, shareholders, and capital. Not because of some conspiracy, because of ownership.

This is why the automation era tends toward concentrated wealth. And concentrated wealth is unstable. Not morally, mechanically.

Because a consumer economy requires consumers. And consumers require purchasing power.

This is the paradox at the heart of automated capitalism: Automation increases efficiency and reduces costs, making goods cheaper and companies more profitable. But if automation also reduces employment, fewer people have income to buy those cheaper goods.

Henry Ford understood this intuitively in the 1910s when he raised wages at his factories. He wasn't being charitable, he was creating customers. Workers who could afford cars became the market for cars. The strategy worked because wage employment was widespread.

The automation era breaks this logic. If machines produce cars and fewer people have wages to buy cars, the market shrinks, unless society finds a new distribution mechanism.

The Early Warning Signs

This isn't hypothetical. We're already seeing early versions of this pattern.

Since the 1980s, the share of GDP going to worker compensation has declined in most developed economies, while the share going to capital has increased. In the United States, labor's share of income dropped from about 64% in the early 2000s to around 58% by 2020.

Meanwhile, corporate profit margins reached historic highs. Stock markets soared. Real estate values in major cities exploded. Asset owners became dramatically wealthier.

But median household income, adjusted for inflation, barely grew. Workers saw their purchasing power stagnate or decline, even as the overall economy expanded.

The automation era will accelerate this pattern. And once it becomes strong enough, the wage system stops functioning as the default distribution mechanism. The economy can no longer distribute purchasing power through employment alone.

The Most Dangerous Outcome: Humiliation

At this point, many people jump straight to the policy debate. Universal basic income. Guaranteed jobs. Social dividends. Tax structures.

We'll get there. But before we talk about policy, we need to talk about psychology.

Because the biggest risk isn't poverty. The biggest risk is humiliation.

A society where millions of people feel unnecessary becomes unstable. Not just economically, emotionally. Because humans can handle hardship. What we struggle with is being treated as irrelevant.

A society can survive a poverty problem. It cannot survive a *humiliation problem* at scale.

This is why the automation era must build not just income systems but dignity systems.

The difference between a stable transition and a chaotic one isn't only money. It's respect. Belonging. Meaning.

Research on long-term unemployment consistently shows that the psychological damage extends far beyond financial stress. Unemployed workers report higher rates of depression, anxiety, and feelings of worthlessness. Suicide rates increase. Marriages strain. Communities fragment.

And this happens even when unemployment benefits provide income. Money alleviates some stress, but it doesn't solve the identity crisis. Work provided more than a paycheck, it provided structure, social connection, status, and purpose.

The automation era risks creating this psychological crisis at scale. Millions of people receiving income but feeling unnecessary. Provided for but not needed. Surviving but not mattering.

That's a recipe for social breakdown.

Why Cheaper Stuff Isn't Enough

A common argument goes like this: 'Automation will make everything cheap. People won't need as much income.'

There's truth here. Automation will collapse costs in many categories: manufactured goods, logistics, some services, certain healthcare diagnostics, educational access, transportation.

But falling prices don't solve everything.

Housing is constrained by land and regulation. Automation can reduce construction costs, but it can't create more land in desirable locations. Healthcare is uneven, diagnostics may become cheaper, but chronic disease management and elder care remain labor-intensive. And humans need stability, not just cheap goods.

A society can't be held together by low prices alone. It must be held together by a stable floor.

The deepest fear in modern life isn't that things are expensive. It's that you'll fall. That you'll become disposable. That you'll lose your place.

Consider someone earning $40,000 per year. If automation makes goods 30% cheaper, their effective purchasing power increases to roughly $52,000 in today's terms. That's meaningful.

But if automation also eliminates their job, they go from $52,000 equivalent to zero. Cheaper goods don't help if you have no income.

The abundance argument only works if it's paired with a distribution mechanism. Otherwise, cheaper goods become inaccessible luxuries for the unemployed.

The New Social Contract

When job income weakens, society faces a redesign. Not optional. Unavoidable. Because instability forces action.

The old contract was: Work to earn the right to live.

The new contract becomes: Citizenship includes the right to stability.

Different nations will experiment differently. Some will expand welfare systems. Some will build universal basic income. Some will create social dividends funded by automation wealth. Some will build job guarantee programs. Some will create hybrid models.

There's no single blueprint. But the direction is unavoidable. Because if the wage system fails, the distribution system must evolve. This isn't ideology, it's mechanical. A society can't remain stable if the majority can't access the wealth the economy produces.

Some examples are already emerging. Alaska's Permanent Fund Dividend provides annual payments to residents funded by oil revenues, a form of resource dividend. Several cities have experimented with guaranteed income pilots. The COVID-19 pandemic led many governments to provide direct cash payments to citizens, demonstrating that universal payments are administratively feasible.

These experiments are small-scale and imperfect, but they demonstrate that societies can build distribution mechanisms beyond wage employment.

A Day in 2040: Maria's Life on Citizens' Dividend

Let me show you what this distribution system looks like when it's wrapped around a real life.

Maria is 42 years old in 2040. Fifteen years ago, she was a legal associate at a mid-sized firm, reviewing contracts and conducting research. AI eliminated that role in 2028. She tried to adapt, worked as a contract attorney, then as a legal consultant, but the demand for human legal work kept declining. By 2035, she'd accepted reality: there was no traditional legal career path anymore.

Now she receives $2,800 monthly from the U.S. Citizens' Dividend, the automation prosperity fund created in 2037 after unemployment hit 14% and political pressure became overwhelming. It's not means-tested. Everyone gets it. It's funded by a combination of corporate automation taxes, data taxes, and dividends from a sovereign AI infrastructure fund.

Maria adds about 10 hours a week of paid work. She helps immigrants navigate legal documentation at a community clinic, and she teaches a small online course on legal ethics. Together with the Dividend, this brings her to roughly $4,000 a month. She works not because she's terrified of missing rent, but because the clinic gives her a reason to get dressed in the morning and the students remind her that what she knows still matters to someone.

Her life isn't luxurious. Rent on her one-bedroom apartment runs $900, kept affordable by automated construction that finally cracked the housing bottleneck. Food costs roughly $350 a month because vertical farms and robotic logistics drove grocery prices down by 60%. A robotaxi ride across town costs about a dollar. Healthcare, transportation, utilities, clothing, none of these categories carry the weight they did fifteen years ago. She saves a little. She eats out sometimes. She took a pottery class last fall and surprised herself by being decent at it.

The floor is real. And for Maria, it holds.

But here's the part people don't like to say out loud: Maria's stability doesn't mean everyone is okay.

Some people adapt the way Maria did. They find the clinic, the pottery class, the small teaching gig that gives Tuesday a shape. Others don't. Maria's neighbor, a former logistics manager named John, has been on the Dividend for three years and mostly watches screens. He isn't hungry. He isn't homeless. But he hasn't left the apartment in four days, and when Maria knocks on his door to invite him to a community dinner, he says he'll think about it. He always says he'll think about it. The Dividend solved his survival. It didn't solve the fact that he used to manage forty people and now he manages nothing. It didn't solve the drinking that started the year the warehouse closed. It didn't solve the quiet fury he carries about a system that provided for him and discarded him in the same motion.

The Dividend solves poverty. It does not automatically solve resentment, addiction, status loss, or the slow erosion of self-respect that comes from feeling unnecessary. That second battle is cultural, not economic. And it is being fought, unevenly and without clear victory, in apartments and community centers and therapy offices across the country.

Maria knows this. She sees it at the clinic, where some clients are rebuilding and others are barely holding on. She sees it in herself on the days when she wonders whether teaching legal ethics to twelve students on a screen is really a life, or just a convincing imitation of one. Most days, she decides it's a life. Some days, she isn't sure. That ambiguity, that unresolved tension between material comfort and existential uncertainty, is the lived reality of the distribution solution. It's better than the alternative. It's not the end of the story.

The Moral Shift Required

This is where the automation era becomes culturally difficult. Because it forces societies to confront a moral evolution:

In the old world, income was tied to labor. In the new world, income becomes tied to citizenship.

This will feel wrong to many people. Not because they're cruel, but because they were raised in a system where work was moral. And work will still be moral. But it will no longer be universal.

The resistance will be strong. People will say: 'Why should anyone get paid for not working?' The answer is complex: Because the economy no longer needs their labor at sufficient scale, and a functional society requires that people can live with dignity whether or not their labor is economically demanded.

This shift echoes earlier moral transformations. Once, child labor was considered normal and necessary. Society evolved. Once, denying women the vote seemed natural. Society evolved. Once, segregation was legal and defended on moral grounds. Society evolved.

The automation era requires a similar evolution: recognizing that in a world of abundance created by machines, income can be decoupled from labor without moral catastrophe.

Building Dignity Systems

Even if income is solved, dignity isn't automatic. A society can provide money and still create humiliation. A society can provide stability and still create emptiness.

So the automation era must build dignity systems. What does that mean?

It means societies must honor contribution beyond employment. Caregiving. Mentorship. Community building. Art. Service. Mastery. These must be socially legitimate. Not treated as hobbies. Not dismissed as laziness.

Consider someone who spends their time caring for an aging parent. In today's system, this person is often economically invisible: no wages, no formal recognition, no career progression. Yet their work is valuable and necessary.

Or consider someone who volunteers extensively in their community: coaching youth sports, organizing food banks, teaching literacy classes. These contributions matter socially, but they don't translate into economic security under the wage system.

The automation era creates space to recognize these forms of contribution. Not because work becomes optional, but because 'work' can be redefined to include what actually matters to communities.

Two Problems At Once

This chapter is about income distribution. But it points directly to something deeper.

Because the wage system wasn't just a distribution system. It was a meaning system. Work gave people a reason to wake up. A sense of progress. A sense of identity.

So when job income weakens, society must solve two problems simultaneously: distribution and purpose. Distribution is the mechanical problem. Purpose is the human problem.

And purpose may be harder. Because money can be delivered through policy. Meaning must be built culturally.

But before we dive into the purpose problem, we need to explore the other side of the equation. Because the automation era isn't only about disruption, it's about abundance. It's about dramatic cost reductions. It's about the possibility that, for the first time in history, the cost of living could collapse.

That's the promise. And it's real.

That's what we explore next.

Chapter 8
The Promise of Abundance

There's a strange habit when we talk about the future. We focus on what will break. What will disappear. What will be disrupted. What will collapse.

Those concerns are valid. The automation era will disrupt jobs. It will reshape industries. It will destabilize the wage system. It will challenge political structures.

Abundance without functional ladders creates a distribution crisis: we have more than enough, but lack the pathways to distribute opportunity.

But if we only talk about disruption, we miss the most powerful force in the entire story.

The automation era isn't only a disruption engine. It's an abundance engine. And abundance is one of the most underestimated forces in human history.

Because abundance does something profound: it reduces desperation. And desperation shapes everything: politics, crime, family stability, mental health, migration, how people treat each other.

Scarcity makes humans sharp, competitive, fearful, tribal. Abundance can soften those edges. Not because humans become angels, but because we become less desperate. And less desperate societies behave differently.

I grew up in a country shaped by both abundance and scarcity existing side by side. Brazil produces enough food to feed its population several times over. It has arable land, fresh water, mineral wealth, human talent. And yet, for most of my childhood, the distribution of that abundance was so unequal that millions lived in poverty beside staggering wealth. I learned early that abundance without distribution is just another form of cruelty. But I also learned that when abundance reaches people, when it actually connects to daily life, it transforms everything. Not perfectly. But unmistakably.

This chapter is about the abundance side of the automation era. The part that could make the future not only richer but kinder.

Why Efficiency Matters So Much

Here's an uncomfortable truth: civilizations rise on efficiency. The societies that can produce more with less tend to dominate. They grow. They stabilize. They expand. They outcompete. Efficiency isn't just a business metric. It's a civilizational force.

The automation era is the most powerful efficiency wave in history because it attacks friction everywhere. AI reduces cognitive friction. Robotics reduces physical friction.

Autonomy reduces transportation friction. Software reduces administrative friction.

Reduce friction across an economy and prices fall. Not all prices. Not evenly. But enough to change daily life.

This is the core mechanism of abundance: automation collapses the cost of production. Lower production costs collapse prices. Collapsed prices raise living standards.

And this isn't theoretical. It's already happened repeatedly in ways we've started taking for granted.

Consider the trajectory of consumer electronics. In the early 1970s, a basic handheld calculator cost the equivalent of over a thousand dollars in today's money. Within two decades, the same functionality cost a few dollars. Today, calculation is effectively free, embedded in every phone and computer. Or communication: international phone calls that once cost dollars per minute are now free video calls across the globe. Or information access: knowledge that once required a trip to a library and a stroke of luck is now instantly available from a device in your pocket.

The automation era extends this pattern from information and communication to physical goods and services.

What Gets Cheaper (And What Doesn't)

When people hear "prices will collapse," they imagine everything becoming cheap overnight. It won't happen like that.

Price collapse will be uneven. The automation era isn't magic. It's economics. It'll reduce costs where labor is a large component, processes can be standardized, and automation can scale.

The biggest cost collapses will likely occur in manufactured goods, logistics and delivery, transportation services, administrative services, educational access through AI tutors, and certain areas of healthcare diagnostics.

But things tied to land, regulation, or social complexity will change slower. Housing. Certain healthcare treatments. Education as a credentialing system. These will evolve, but not instantly.

Take housing. Construction costs could drop significantly through automation: robotic fabrication, 3D-printed structures, modular assembly. But land prices in desirable locations won't drop. Zoning regulations won't automatically change. So housing abundance will be geographically uneven.

Or higher education. AI tutors can make learning nearly free. But college degrees are credentialing systems as much as learning systems. The perceived value of an elite degree won't collapse just because online learning becomes excellent. Status goods resist price collapse.

The Solar Panel That Changed Everything

Let me show you what automation-driven abundance looks like in practice.

In 2010, solar panels were expensive. Installing a typical residential system cost tens of thousands of dollars before subsidies. Solar power was a luxury, something environmentally conscious wealthy homeowners could afford, but economically irrational for most people.

By the mid-2020s, manufacturing costs had dropped by roughly 95%. The same system that was prohibitively expensive a decade and a half earlier had become affordable for middle-class homeowners in many markets.

What happened? Automation.

Manufacturers, particularly in Asia, achieved this through massive automation of the production process. Robots now handle wafer cutting, cell assembly, module lamination, quality inspection, and packaging. A modern solar panel factory operates with a fraction of the workforce required in 2010, while producing many times as many panels per square foot of factory space.

The result isn't only cheaper panels. It's a fundamental shift in global energy economics.

Solar power is now the cheapest form of new electricity generation in most of the world. Not because of subsidies or environmental mandates, but because of economics. The cost per unit of solar electricity has fallen below coal, natural gas, and in many regions, even existing nuclear power. This happened faster than almost anyone projected.

The implications extend far beyond electricity bills. Developing nations that couldn't afford to build traditional power plants can now deploy solar at scale. Countries across sub-Saharan Africa and rural Asia have brought electricity to millions of people through distributed solar installations. Climate change mitigation became economically rational, not just morally urgent, because clean energy is now cheaper than dirty energy in most contexts.

Yes, automation displaced workers in solar manufacturing. Factories that once employed hundreds now employ dozens. But those dozens produce enough panels to power hundreds of thousands of homes. The productivity gain is extraordinary.

The solar story illustrates what abundance actually means: not that everyone gets rich, but that things that were once expensive or impossible become cheap and accessible. It means solving problems at scale that were previously intractable.

And solar is just one example. The same pattern appears across automated manufacturing: LED lighting, lithium batteries, computer memory, telecommunications equipment. Automation drives costs down, making advanced technology accessible to billions rather than millions.

This is the promise of the automation era. Not utopia, but genuine material abundance that creates previously impossible solutions to humanity's challenges.

When Services Become Software

One of the most profound changes AI introduces is this: many services become software.

For most of human history, services were expensive because they required human attention. A lawyer. A tutor. An accountant. A consultant. A designer. A customer service agent. These roles were costly not because humans are greedy, but because humans require time. And time is scarce.

AI changes this by delivering analysis, tutoring, planning, translation, and coordination at near-zero marginal cost. This isn't the end of professionals, but it changes the baseline. It makes competence more accessible.

Consider legal services. A basic will drafted by a lawyer might cost well over a thousand dollars. AI-powered legal services can now produce legally valid documents for a fraction of that. The quality isn't identical. Complex estates still need human lawyers. But for straightforward cases, the cost collapses.

Or language tutoring. A human tutor might charge the equivalent of a nice dinner per hour. An AI tutor provides unlimited practice, instant correction, personalized lessons, and adaptive difficulty for the cost of a streaming subscription per month. The human tutor still offers something irreplaceable: cultural context, encouragement, relationship. But the baseline cost of language learning plummets.

I think about this in terms of what it would have meant for my parents' generation in Brazil. Access to a good English tutor was a class marker. Families that could afford it gave their children an economic advantage that compounded for decades. The families that couldn't were locked out. AI tutoring doesn't eliminate that inequality overnight. But it breaks the lock. A kid in a small town in Santa Catarina can now access language instruction that rivals what wealthy families in São Paulo could buy. That's not a small thing.

The Hidden Savings in Logistics

Logistics is one of the hidden costs of modern life. We pay for it in grocery prices, online delivery, retail, manufacturing, healthcare supply chains, every physical product.

Logistics is expensive because it's complex: warehouses, inventory, shipping, sorting, last-mile delivery, returns, storage. But robotics and AI thrive in logistics. It's measurable, repetitive, optimization-friendly.

Warehouses become robot cities. Sorting becomes automated. Delivery becomes more efficient. The result: physical goods become cheaper. Not because the goods themselves improve, but because moving them gets cheaper.

In a typical product sold online, the logistics component, warehousing, sorting, packaging, shipping, can account for a third or more of the final price. When automation reduces those logistics costs substantially, even by 30 or 40 percent, the savings multiply across millions of products and billions of transactions. The aggregate impact on household budgets becomes significant.

Transportation as a Utility

Transportation isn't just an industry. It's a cost layer on top of every industry. When transportation becomes autonomous, transportation costs fall. And when transportation costs fall, everything else becomes cheaper.

But transportation is also one of the most psychologically important shifts because it changes daily life.

Imagine a world where robotaxis are cheap, autonomous buses run continuously, delivery is fast and low-cost, and trucking is efficient. Transportation becomes closer to a utility, like electricity, like internet. Something you access, not something you own.

This changes cities, commuting, parking, urban design, and the cost of living.

Consider car ownership costs. The average American household spends thousands of dollars per year on car ownership: payments, insurance, maintenance, fuel, parking. For many families, transportation is the second-largest expense after housing.

If autonomous ride-sharing becomes sufficiently cheap and convenient, many urban households could abandon car ownership entirely. Instead of paying for a car that sits idle most of the day, they might spend a fraction of that amount on unlimited autonomous rides. The difference goes directly back into household budgets. For a median-income family, that's a meaningful increase in effective purchasing power.

Education Access Explodes

Education has always been constrained by scarcity. Not scarcity of information. Scarcity of teaching. A great teacher can only teach so many students. A tutor is expensive. A mentor is rare.

AI tutors collapse this scarcity. This is one of the most hopeful forms of abundance, because education is one of the strongest levers for human potential.

AI tutors make personalized learning, adaptive practice, and unlimited explanation available to millions. This raises the ceiling of human learning. But more importantly: it raises the floor.

Because many students aren't incapable. They're unsupported.

Consider a child struggling with algebra. In a typical classroom, the teacher has thirty students and forty-five minutes. If this child needs extra explanation, they might get five minutes of attention. Not enough to truly understand. In previous generations, this child would simply fall behind.

With an AI tutor, this child has unlimited patience. The tutor can explain the same concept fifteen different ways. It can generate practice problems at exactly the right difficulty level. It can identify precisely which prerequisite concept the child is missing. It can work at 10 PM when homework frustration peaks.

This doesn't replace human teachers. It amplifies them. Teachers can focus on motivation, creativity, and social-emotional learning while AI handles the repetitive explanation and practice.

Healthcare's Uneven Revolution

Healthcare abundance will arrive unevenly, but where it arrives, it'll be transformative.

AI diagnostics are already performing at or above human levels at certain tasks: reading medical images, detecting patterns in pathology, predicting drug interactions, identifying early disease markers.

Wearable devices can now monitor heart rhythms continuously. AI algorithms can detect irregular patterns, early signs of cardiac conditions, weeks or months before symptoms appear.

Early detection means early treatment. Early treatment means avoiding emergency room visits, bypassing expensive surgeries, preventing strokes. The cost of continuous monitoring is modest. The cost of emergency cardiac care is enormous. The savings, both human and financial, are transformative.

Or consider diabetes management. Continuous glucose monitors paired with AI can predict blood sugar fluctuations hours in advance, helping diabetics avoid dangerous episodes. Better management means fewer hospitalizations, fewer complications, lower long-term healthcare costs.

Healthcare abundance will be uneven at first. Diagnostic tools will improve faster than treatment infrastructure. Prevention will advance faster than cures. But the direction is powerful.

What Abundance Actually Feels Like

Abundance isn't only numbers. It's psychological. When essentials become cheaper, people feel different. When survival anxiety declines, societies behave differently.

Abundance changes crime rates, stress levels, family stability, mental health, political extremism, and social trust. Not perfectly. Not automatically. But meaningfully.

Research on poverty and decision-making has shown this clearly. When people are struggling financially, their cognitive bandwidth narrows. They make worse long-term decisions not because they're less intelligent, but because scarcity creates constant mental stress that impairs judgment.

Remove that stress, even partially, and behavior changes. People save more. They invest in education. They plan further ahead. They treat others better. They engage more in civic life.

Studies of basic income experiments consistently show this pattern. When people receive guaranteed income, employment rates don't collapse. Most people continue working. But health outcomes improve. Children perform better in school. Domestic violence decreases. Crime rates drop.

Abundance, even modest abundance, changes societies at the behavioral level.

The Abundance Paradox

Now we arrive at the paradox. Abundance is good. But abundance also creates a new risk.

Because humans don't only need resources. Humans need meaning.

In a scarce world, meaning is often forced. You work to survive. You struggle. You build. You endure. Scarcity provides structure. Abundance removes structure. And structure matters.

This is why abundance can create emptiness. Not because abundance is bad, but because humans aren't designed for unlimited comfort without purpose.

Research on sudden wealth consistently shows that many people who receive large windfalls end up unhappy. The initial euphoria fades. Relationships strain. Purpose evaporates. Without the structure of work or the motivation of striving, many drift.

Or consider retirement. Many people spend decades looking forward to it: freedom from work schedules, time to pursue interests. Yet research shows retirement often brings unexpected challenges. Some retirees thrive. Others struggle. Without the structure of work, days feel aimless. Social connections weaken. Identity erodes.

The automation era risks creating this psychology at scale. Not through sudden windfalls, but through gradual displacement. Resources without purpose. Time without meaning.

Cheap Doesn't Mean Happy

It's tempting to imagine that if everything becomes cheap, society becomes joyful. But humans aren't purely economic creatures. We're status creatures. Identity creatures. Belonging creatures. Meaning creatures.

A world where everything is cheap could still be a world where people are miserable. Because meaning isn't purchased. Meaning is built.

We can see this pattern in wealthy societies today. Some of the most materially comfortable nations on Earth, countries with strong social safety nets, low poverty, and high living standards, also report significant rates of depression, antidepressant use, and mental health challenges. Abundance alone doesn't guarantee happiness.

Conversely, some communities with modest material wealth report high life satisfaction when they have strong social bonds, clear purpose, and meaningful roles. Humans thrive on challenge, contribution, and connection as much as comfort.

The Most Important Abundance: Time

The most radical form of abundance isn't cheap goods. It's time.

Automation reduces the labor required to run society. That means humans will have more time. Sometimes through freedom. Sometimes through displacement. But the total time demanded by survival labor declines.

Time is a gift. But time is also a burden. Because time requires self-direction. And self-direction is hard.

The automation era will create a society where some people flourish with freedom, and some people collapse into drift. This is why purpose becomes central. Because time without meaning becomes emptiness.

The Distraction Trap

The easiest way to fill time is distraction. And modern civilization is already brilliant at it.

The automation era will make distraction more powerful. AI will personalize entertainment. Algorithms will optimize attention capture. Virtual worlds will become more immersive. Content will become endless.

A society with more free time and more powerful entertainment risks becoming a society of passive consumption. And passive consumption isn't fulfillment. It's sedation.

We already see early versions of this. The average person in a developed country now spends a remarkable portion of their waking hours on screens: television, social media, streaming, gaming. Much of this is passive consumption. And research increasingly links excessive screen time to anxiety, depression, and decreased life satisfaction.

The automation era amplifies this risk. Abundance without purpose creates fertile ground for distraction. And distraction without limit creates populations that are comfortable but unfulfilled.

Abundance Changes Everything

Abundance is the promise of automation. Cheaper goods. Better services. More access. Less desperation. These are real gifts.

But abundance also changes global power. Because if production becomes automated, nations become less dependent on cheap labor abroad. Supply chains shorten. Factories move closer to consumers. And the old advantage of cheap-labor countries begins to weaken.

This is one of the most dramatic shifts of the automation era.

It reshapes globalization. And globalization shaped the last fifty years. The automation era will reshape the next fifty.

That's what we explore next.

Chapter 9

When Cheap Labor Stops Mattering

For the last half-century, globalization ran on a simple equation: move production to where labor is cheapest.

That equation shaped everything. Factories moved to Asia. Supply chains stretched across oceans. Developing nations industrialized. Middle classes rose in places that had once been poor. Consumers in wealthy nations enjoyed cheaper goods. Corporations increased profits. Global trade expanded.

The modern world was built on the idea that labor costs mattered more than distance. And for decades, that was true.

But the automation era introduces a new equation. A more disruptive one. Because when robots do the work, labor cost stops being the primary advantage. And when labor cost stops being the primary advantage, the global economy reorganizes.

I think about this differently than most technology writers because I grew up on one end of this equation. Brazil industrialized through exactly this playbook. Foreign capital arrived because labor was cheap. Factories opened in São

Paulo, in Manaus, in the industrial belt of the south. My parents' generation built lives around the jobs those factories created. The arrangement was never equitable, the profits flowed disproportionately to the capital owners, but the jobs were real. They built a middle class. They gave families like mine a foothold. The automation era threatens to pull that foothold away, not just in Brazil, but everywhere the development ladder depended on the value of human labor.

This chapter is about one of the most underestimated shifts of the automation era: the slow collapse of cheap labor as a national superpower.

Why Cheap Labor Was Everything

Cheap labor isn't simply "low wages." It's leverage. A country with cheap labor could offer the world something priceless: the ability to produce goods at a lower cost.

This allowed developing nations to attract manufacturing. Manufacturing created jobs. Jobs created income. Income created domestic demand. Domestic demand created growth. Growth created stability.

This is how nations climbed. This is how East Asia transformed over the past fifty years. This is how Southeast Asia expanded. This is how parts of Latin America industrialized. This is how the global middle class grew.

Consider the trajectory of the countries that followed this path most successfully. Nations that were overwhelmingly agricultural and deeply poor in the 1970s and 1980s opened their economies, attracted foreign investment, and leveraged their greatest asset: large populations willing to work for wages that seemed impossibly low by Western standards. Within a generation or two, hundreds of millions of people escaped extreme poverty. Urban middle classes expanded. Infrastructure modernized. Living standards rose dramatically.

The formula wasn't unique. Across East Asia, Southeast Asia, and pockets of Latin America and South Asia, variations of the same playbook produced similar results: leverage cheap labor to attract manufacturing, use manufacturing to build capital, use capital to climb the value chain.

Cheap labor wasn't just an advantage. It was the ladder. The industrial ladder. The pathway from poverty to prosperity.

The automation era weakens that ladder. Because robots don't demand wages.

The Robot Has No Nationality

Here's the key insight: a robot doesn't become cheaper because it's placed in a poorer country. A robot costs roughly the same everywhere.

The robot may be slightly cheaper to operate in a nation with cheaper energy. But labor cost is no longer the main variable. And that changes everything.

In the old world, labor cost differences created massive incentives to outsource production. A factory worker in the United States might earn ten times what a factory worker in Vietnam or Bangladesh earns. For labor-intensive manufacturing, textiles, electronics assembly, anything requiring significant human handling, this gap was decisive.

Even accounting for shipping costs, quality control challenges, and longer supply chains, the savings were enormous.

But when an industrial robot operates for a decade after a single capital expenditure, location becomes less relevant. The robot's annual operating cost, mainly electricity and maintenance, varies only modestly between countries. Suddenly, the cost differential between manufacturing in Ohio and manufacturing in Hanoi isn't tenfold. It's maybe ten or fifteen percent. And that smaller gap gets overwhelmed by other factors: shipping costs, supply chain resilience, time-to-market, geopolitical risk.

In the automation era, those incentives weaken. Because if labor isn't the cost driver, distance becomes more important again. Supply chain risk becomes more important. Political stability becomes more important. Energy becomes more important.

The advantage stack shifts.

The Great Reversal: Factories Return Home

If you no longer need large workforces, why build a factory on the other side of the planet?

Why deal with long shipping routes, geopolitical risk, supply chain fragility, tariffs, and time delays?

If a factory is mostly robots, you can build it closer to the consumer market. You can build it in North America. In Europe. In wealthy regions. You can shorten supply chains. Reduce shipping. Reduce inventory costs. Reduce risk.

The automation era encourages a reversal: production returns closer to consumption. Not completely. Not instantly. But meaningfully.

We're already seeing early signs. Governments in the United States, Europe, Japan, and South Korea are investing heavily in domestic semiconductor fabrication, bringing cutting-edge chip production back after decades of offshoring. The decisions aren't driven by cheap domestic labor, there is none, but by automation capability, government subsidies, and supply chain security concerns exposed by recent disruptions.

Similarly, several major consumer goods companies have experimented with highly automated factories in high-wage countries, returning production that had been offshore for decades. Some of these experiments have succeeded. Others have stalled for reasons unrelated to the core economics. But the principle is clear: automation enables reshoring.

This is one of the reasons the automation era will reshape geopolitics. Because global dependence declines. And global dependence was one of the stabilizing forces of globalization.

When nations depend on each other for goods, trade becomes a peace mechanism. Economic interdependence creates mutual interest in stability. War becomes economically irrational when your adversary manufactures your products.

When nations can produce locally through automation, dependence declines. And when dependence declines, geopolitical tension can rise. The economic ties that constrained conflict weaken.

The Developing Nation Trap

Now we reach the uncomfortable part.

Many developing nations built their entire growth model on cheap labor. They attracted factories. They created jobs. They built export economies. They climbed the development ladder.

Automation changes this equation. Because the factories of the future don't require as many humans.

A developing nation may still attract manufacturing. But it may attract capital investment, machines, output, and exports without attracting jobs at the same scale. This is the developing nation trap: a world where industrialization no longer produces mass employment. Where nations can't climb through labor.

Consider garment manufacturing, one of the classic first rungs on the development ladder. Countries across South and Southeast Asia built economies on textile exports, employing millions of workers, supporting tens of millions of family members. It's the textbook case of leveraging cheap labor to create jobs and build capital.

But garment manufacturing is increasingly automatable. Sewing robots are improving. AI systems can optimize cutting patterns to minimize waste. Automated quality inspection reduces the need for human checkers. A factory that once employed thousands of workers might employ hundreds in a highly automated configuration.

Countries that depend on this industry face a cruel choice: if they automate, they maintain export competitiveness but lose job creation. If they don't automate, they lose competitiveness to countries that do, or to reshored production in wealthy nations.

Either path is difficult. This is the trap.

This is one of the most destabilizing possibilities of the automation era: it creates a global divide not just between individuals, but between nations. Countries that industrialized in the 20th century had decades to build middle classes through manufacturing employment. Countries trying to industrialize in the 21st century may find that window closing.

I feel the weight of this personally. Brazil is caught in the middle. It industrialized enough to build a middle class but not enough to become a technology leader. It has the institutional capacity to adopt automation but not the capital depth to lead it. It has cheap energy through hydroelectric and solar potential, but it has governance challenges that slow deployment. The automation era could go either way for Brazil. It could leapfrog, leveraging its energy abundance and educated workforce. Or it could stall, trapped between wealthy nations that automate faster and poorer nations that undercut on whatever manual labor remains. The same uncertainty applies to dozens of middle-income countries. And the outcome depends less on technology than on political choices made in the next decade.

The New Advantage Stack

If cheap labor weakens, what becomes the new advantage?

Automation rewards a different set of national strengths:

Energy abundance. Robots run on electricity. Datacenters run on electricity. AI is fundamentally an energy industry. Nations with cheap, abundant energy gain advantage. Countries with hydroelectric, geothermal, nuclear, or strong solar and wind resources find themselves newly advantaged, regardless of their labor costs.

Political stability. Automation infrastructure is capital-intensive. Investors prefer stable environments. Nations with instability lose investment. Building a multi-billion dollar automated manufacturing facility requires confidence in decades of stability. Weak rule of law, corruption, political volatility, these create risk premiums that make investment uneconomical.

Capital access. Automation requires upfront investment: robots, factories, datacenters, infrastructure. Nations with access to deep capital markets, institutional investors, and banking systems that can finance large-scale projects adopt faster. Developing nations often lack this infrastructure, creating a barrier to adoption that compounds over time.

Compute ecosystems. AI requires chips, datacenters, networks, talent. Nations that control compute supply chains gain power. The semiconductor supply chain is already one of the most concentrated and strategically sensitive in the world. Control over compute infrastructure is becoming a strategic asset comparable to oil in the 20th century.

Regulatory speed. Slow adoption creates disadvantage. Fast adoption compounds. Nations that can quickly permit autonomous vehicle testing, approve AI medical diagnostics, and deploy automated infrastructure gain first-mover advantages. Bureaucratic friction becomes a competitive liability.

This is why the automation era isn't only about technology. It's about national capability.

From Cheap to Capable

For decades, developing nations were described as "cheap labor countries." This narrative shaped global power, investment, migration, and national identity.

Automation changes this narrative. A nation can't rely on being cheap. It must rely on being capable.

This is a harsh transition. Because capability is harder to build than cheapness. Cheapness is an accident of wages. Capability requires education, infrastructure, stability, and governance.

This is why the automation era will widen the gap between nations. Because capability compounds. And compounding creates divergence.

Consider two countries starting from similar positions. One has strong institutions, good infrastructure, and higher wages. The other has weak institutions but cheap labor. In the 20th century, the second country could compete by attracting labor-intensive manufacturing. In the automation era, the first country deploys robots, automated logistics, AI systems. Its productivity soars. It produces more with fewer people. Its citizens enjoy rising living standards. Its government collects more revenue to invest in further automation.

The second country, lacking capital and institutions, can't automate as quickly. Its cheap labor advantage erodes. Manufacturing moves elsewhere. Growth stalls.

The gap widens. Not because the second country's people are less capable, but because the structure of global competition has changed.

The Migration Pressure That's Coming

When cheap labor loses its advantage, developing nations may face fewer jobs, slower wage growth, and more instability. Migration pressure increases. Not because people are lazy, because people seek opportunity. If the ladder breaks, people move.

This creates political tension in developed nations. Because developed nations will simultaneously face workforce disruption at home and migration pressure from abroad. This combination is politically explosive.

Imagine a working-class community in a wealthy nation. Local manufacturing has declined due to automation. Employment is thinning. Then migration increases as people from developing nations seek opportunity. The perception, accurate or not, is that outsiders are competing for scarce resources while locals are suffering.

This breeds resentment. Populist movements gain strength. Nationalist rhetoric intensifies. Democratic norms strain.

We've seen early versions of this pattern in recent years, across Europe, the United States, and elsewhere. The automation era may intensify it considerably.

The Inverse Impact

The automation era creates what I call the inverse impact.

Developed nations become less dependent on imports. They can produce more locally. They can automate factories. They can shorten supply chains. This reduces demand for cheap labor abroad.

Developing nations lose export opportunities. And this isn't just economic. It's social. Because export-driven growth supported rising wages, expanding middle classes, and political stability. When export growth weakens, stability weakens.

This is why the automation era risks creating a world of abundance islands surrounded by instability. And that world isn't stable. Not for anyone.

Consider the global supply chain for consumer electronics. Currently, much of it flows through East Asia: components manufactured and assembled across multiple countries, then shipped globally. This created millions of jobs and lifted entire regions.

If automation enables wealthy nations to produce electronics domestically, or if a few highly automated hubs dominate production, the regional spillover effects disappear. The jobs vanish. The growth engine stops. Those displaced populations don't disappear. They become sources of instability, within their countries and potentially beyond.

The Hope: Leapfrogging

Now we must address the hopeful possibility. Automation isn't only a threat to developing nations. It's also a tool.

AI tutors can improve education. AI healthcare can improve access. Robotics can improve agriculture. Autonomous logistics can improve infrastructure. Digital money can expand commerce. Developing nations could leapfrog.

Just as mobile phones allowed many developing countries to skip landline infrastructure entirely, AI and automation could allow leapfrogging of certain development stages. Some African nations became global leaders in mobile payments precisely because they lacked extensive banking infrastructure. The absence of legacy systems became an advantage.

I've seen this dynamic firsthand through my work at Circle. Stablecoins and digital payments are already reaching populations that traditional banking never served. In parts of Africa, Latin America, and Southeast Asia, people who never had bank accounts now have access to dollar-denominated digital money, instant transfers, and financial services that would have been impossible a decade ago. The technology leapfrogged the banks. The same pattern could play out across education, healthcare, and agriculture, if the institutional foundations are in place.

But leapfrogging requires institutions. And institutions are hard. It requires functioning government, rule of law, property rights, contract enforcement, stable currency, reliable electricity, internet infrastructure.

These aren't trivial prerequisites. They're the foundations of state capacity. And building state capacity takes decades. This is why the automation era isn't only about technology. It's about governance.

The Strategic Question

In the automation era, nations face a new strategic question: do we compete on labor or do we compete on capability?

Labor competition is weakening. Capability competition is rising. This shifts national priorities toward education, energy, compute, and infrastructure. The nations that build these systems will dominate. The nations that can't will struggle.

This is the new global hierarchy.

The end of cheap labor isn't only an economic shift. It's a geopolitical shift. It changes trade. It changes alliances. It changes national leverage. It changes the global balance of power.

As automation spreads, the world won't become more equal. It'll become more unequal between fast adopters and slow adopters. This is the new divide. And it may become the defining geopolitical story of the century.

That divide, and what it means for global power, is what we explore next.

Chapter 10
The New Global Divide

The automation era doesn't arrive evenly. It never could.

Technology doesn't spread like water. It spreads like fire. It ignites where conditions are favorable. It accelerates where incentives are strong. It stalls where institutions are weak. And it leaves behind regions that can't adapt fast enough.

This is why the automation era won't simply change jobs and prices. It'll reshape global power.

The nations that adopt automation fastest will compound advantages. They'll become more productive, more self-sufficient, more economically resilient, and more strategically powerful. The nations that adopt slowly will fall behind. Not gradually. Exponentially.

The global divide doesn't arrive all at once. It unfolds across phases. In the near term, the gaps begin to show as early-adopting nations and companies pull ahead while others lag. Over the following decade, the divide becomes stark and politically explosive as automation-rich nations achieve abundance while automation-poor nations face economic stagnation. By the 2040s, the world risks splitting into two distinct economic realities: automated prosperity and manual poverty. Understanding this timeline matters because the window to prevent the worst outcomes exists primarily now, in the early phase of adoption.

This is the new global divide. And it may become one of the most destabilizing forces of the century.

From Industrial to Computational

For the last two centuries, global power was shaped by industrialization. Nations that industrialized first became empires. Britain led the first industrial revolution and dominated the 19th century. The United States industrialized massively in the late 1800s and dominated the 20th. Nations that industrialized later rose to prosperity. Nations that failed to industrialize remained poor and dependent.

The industrial divide was about factories, railroads, oil, steel production, and mass manufacturing capability.

The automation era creates a new divide. Not industrial. Computational.

The automation divide is about AI capability, robotics deployment, energy abundance, chip supply chains, datacenter infrastructure, and institutional speed.

This isn't a moral divide. It's a compounding divide. Because automation rewards those who can scale it. And scaling requires infrastructure that takes years or decades to build.

Consider the parallel to railroads in the 1800s. Nations that built extensive rail networks gained enormous economic advantages. Moving goods and people became cheaper and faster. Commerce expanded. Industries flourished. These nations pulled ahead of those without rail infrastructure, and the gap persisted for generations.

The automation divide works similarly. Nations that build AI infrastructure, deploy robotics, invest in compute, these nations will pull ahead. And once ahead, they compound their advantage.

Adoption Speed as a National Weapon

In the automation era, adoption speed isn't a business advantage. It's a national weapon.

The nations that deploy AI and robotics quickly will reduce costs, increase productivity, and strengthen their economies. This creates more wealth. More wealth funds more infrastructure. More infrastructure accelerates adoption. This is compounding. Compounding creates divergence.

A nation that's ahead by a modest margin today can be ahead by a dramatic margin tomorrow. Not because it's smarter. Because it's compounding.

Consider two nations starting from similar positions. One invests heavily in automation infrastructure: datacenters, robotics manufacturing, AI research, energy systems. The other delays due to political dysfunction, capital constraints, or regulatory hesitation.

Within five years, the first nation's cumulative productivity advantage is substantial. Its greater wealth allows more investment. The second nation, now falling behind, struggles to afford the infrastructure investments the first nation made years earlier.

Within a decade, the gap may be nearly uncloseable through normal means. The first nation's citizens enjoy higher living standards, better services, more opportunity. Its government has more revenue to invest. The second nation faces brain drain as talented citizens emigrate. Path dependence takes hold.

This is exponential divergence. And it happens not because one nation's people are less capable, but because compounding advantages create structural separation.

The Four Pillars of Automation Power

In the automation era, national power rests on four pillars:

Compute. AI requires chips, datacenters, networks. The nations that control compute supply chains have leverage. Compute becomes a strategic resource comparable to oil or nuclear capability. The semiconductor supply chain is already one of the most concentrated and contested in the world. Advanced chip fabrication is dominated by a handful of facilities, mostly in East Asia. Design capability is concentrated in a few Western companies. This concentration creates vulnerability and leverage simultaneously. Nations increasingly view chip production as national security infrastructure, and the competition to onshore fabrication capacity is intensifying.

Energy. AI is an energy industry. Robots run on electricity. Datacenters require massive power. Nations with cheap, abundant energy gain advantage. Energy abundance becomes a competitive moat. A large AI datacenter can consume as much electricity as a small city. Training a single large AI model can use electricity equivalent to hundreds of homes for a year. As AI scales, energy becomes the limiting constraint. Nations with cheap, reliable electricity have structural advantages regardless of their historical economic position.

Capital. Automation requires investment: robots, factories, infrastructure. The nations with access to capital can deploy faster. A cutting-edge chip fabrication facility costs billions to build. Deploying nationwide autonomous vehicle infrastructure requires hundreds of billions. Only nations with deep capital markets and strong credit can finance these projects. This creates a catch-22 for developing nations: they need automation to grow, but they lack the capital to automate. Wealthy nations can borrow cheaply to invest in productivity-enhancing automation, further widening the gap.

Institutions. This is the most underestimated pillar. Institutions determine whether a nation can build infrastructure, educate citizens, regulate wisely, and maintain stability. Technology doesn't thrive in chaos. It thrives in systems. Strong property rights, enforceable contracts, predictable regulation, university research systems, and cultural acceptance of experimentation, these are the conditions that allow automation to take root. Nations with weak institutions, corruption, political instability, and arbitrary regulation will struggle to deploy automation effectively even if they have access to the technology.

The Rise of Self-Sufficient Nations

One of the most dramatic effects of automation is this: nations become less dependent on imports.

If manufacturing becomes automated, production can return closer to consumers. If energy becomes abundant through solar and nuclear, dependence on foreign energy declines. If supply chains shorten, vulnerability declines.

This creates a world where wealthy nations can become more self-sufficient. This isn't isolationism. It's structural. It's the natural consequence of automation.

And it changes geopolitics. Because global dependence was one of the stabilizing forces of the last half-century.

When nations depend on each other, trade becomes a peace mechanism. The European Union was built partly on this principle: make war economically irrational through interdependence. When nations can produce locally, dependence declines. And when dependence declines, strategic competition can rise. The economic ties that constrained conflict weaken.

This doesn't mean war becomes inevitable. But it removes one stabilizing mechanism that moderated tensions during the globalization era.

The Africa Question

Consider the impact on sub-Saharan Africa. The region has a young, rapidly growing population of over a billion people with a median age under 20. The traditional development path would be industrialization: attract manufacturing, create jobs, build a middle class.

But if automation eliminates the labor advantage, that path narrows or closes. Manufacturing might return to wealthy nations or concentrate in a few highly automated hubs. Africa's demographic dividend, hundreds of millions of young workers, could become a demographic burden if jobs don't materialize.

A billion young people without economic opportunity isn't a stable scenario. It creates pressure that manifests as migration, conflict, or political upheaval.

This is not a distant abstraction for me. I work at a company that builds financial infrastructure for exactly these populations. I've seen the data on remittance flows, on mobile money adoption, on the hunger for economic participation in places where traditional institutions have failed to deliver it. The energy is there. The ambition is there. What's uncertain is whether the global economic structure will provide a ladder, or whether automation will pull it away before these populations can climb.

The Migration Pressure Wave

Migration is one of the most emotionally charged issues in modern politics. The automation era intensifies it.

Developing nations may face fewer jobs, weaker export growth, and rising instability. Meanwhile, developed nations may face workforce disruption, wage stagnation, and cultural anxiety.

This combination is explosive. Because migration becomes both a humanitarian issue and a political weapon.

A society that feels economically insecure becomes less welcoming. Not because people become cruel, but because insecurity makes humans defensive.

We've already seen preview versions of this dynamic. Populist movements across Europe and the Americas have gained strength by combining anti-immigration rhetoric with economic nationalism. The automation era could intensify this pattern: push factors from developing nations increase as opportunity shrinks, pull factors to developed nations persist, but receiving nations face their own economic disruption, creating political backlash.

The New Arms Race

The automation era creates a new arms race. Not only military. Economic.

The race is about AI capability, robotics manufacturing, chip supply chains, energy infrastructure, and datacenter dominance. This race will shape alliances, trade policies, industrial strategy, and national security.

The nations that control these systems will have leverage. The nations that don't will become dependent. This is a new form of power projection. Not territorial. Technological.

Consider the current competition between the world's two largest economies. It's not primarily about military bases or territory. It's about semiconductor supply chains, AI research leadership, network infrastructure, quantum computing capability, and control over emerging technology standards.

Both understand that leadership in automation technologies translates to economic and military power. One has announced explicit national plans targeting dominance in AI, robotics, and advanced manufacturing. The other responds with industrial policy, export controls, and massive research investment.

This competition shapes global alliances. Other major powers must choose whether to align with one technology ecosystem or build independent capability. Smaller nations face pressure to pick sides. Technology becomes inseparable from geopolitics.

The Abundance Islands Problem

The automation era risks creating abundance islands: regions where costs collapse, productivity rises, healthcare improves, education becomes personalized, and wealth compounds. Surrounded by regions where jobs decline, wages stagnate, institutions weaken, and instability rises.

This isn't a stable world. Because instability doesn't stay contained. It spreads through migration, conflict, economic shocks, and political contagion.

A world of abundance islands surrounded by chaos isn't a good future. Even for the wealthy. Because chaos eventually reaches everyone.

History provides examples. Gated communities exist within unstable cities, but the instability eventually affects everyone, through crime spillover, economic disruption, or social breakdown. Wealthy nations in an unstable world face similar dynamics: refugee crises, terrorism, economic volatility, pandemic spread.

True stability requires broad-based prosperity, not isolated abundance. The automation era tests whether humanity can build systems that create widespread benefit rather than concentrated advantage.

The Leapfrogging Possibility

The automation era isn't only a threat to developing nations. It's also a tool. AI tutors can improve education. AI healthcare can improve access. Robotics can improve agriculture. Autonomous logistics can improve infrastructure. Digital money can expand commerce.

Developing nations could leapfrog. Just as mobile phones allowed many countries to skip landline infrastructure, automation could allow skipping of certain development stages. Nations without entrenched industrial systems might adopt automated agriculture, AI education, and digital commerce faster than nations with established but inefficient traditional systems.

But leapfrogging requires institutions. And institutions are hard. It requires functioning government, rule of law, property rights, contract enforcement, stable currency, reliable electricity, internet infrastructure.

These aren't trivial prerequisites. They're the foundations of state capacity. And building state capacity takes decades. Technology doesn't replace governance. It amplifies it. A nation can have access to AI tools and still fail to improve if corruption, instability, or weak institutions prevent adoption.

The exceptions exist. Small nations with strong governance have demonstrated that good institutions can enable technological leapfrogging even with limited resources. But exceptions don't make a pattern. Most developing nations struggle with institutional capacity. And the automation era rewards institutional quality more than any previous technological wave.

What Shapes Everything

The new global divide will be shaped by many factors: compute, capital, institutions. But underneath all of these lies one foundation that matters more than anything else: energy.

Not only because energy powers robots. But because energy powers compute. And compute powers AI. Energy becomes the throttle of the entire automation era.

This is why energy becomes destiny. And this is why the future may not only be built on Earth. Because the most abundant energy source in human history isn't underground. It's overhead. The sun.

And once you take the sun seriously, a new idea becomes plausible: space as infrastructure. Space as energy. Space as the foundation of the new economy.

It sounds like science fiction. But the automation era makes it economics.

That's what we explore next.

Chapter 11

Energy as Destiny

If the automation era has a hidden foundation, it's energy. Not because energy is exciting, but because energy is everything.

Robots run on electricity. Datacenters run on electricity. Autonomous vehicles run on electricity. AI systems run on electricity. Factories run on electricity.

The future economy isn't only an intelligence economy. It's an energy economy.

This is one of the most important truths in this entire book: AI is an energy industry.

And once you understand that, the automation era becomes clearer. Because it reveals what will matter most: energy abundance, energy cost, energy reliability, and energy sovereignty.

I started thinking about energy differently a few years ago, when I got involved in Bitcoin mining through one of our family businesses. Mining is computationally intensive and energy-hungry, and it forces you to think about electricity the way most people think about rent: as the single largest line item that determines whether the whole operation is viable. That experience gave me a visceral understanding of something most technology discussions treat as an abstraction. Compute is energy. Intelligence is energy. The automation economy runs on watts before it runs on algorithms.

Why Energy Becomes the Core Constraint

For most of modern history, the world was constrained by labor. Labor was scarce. Labor was expensive. Labor limited output.

The automation era changes this. Labor becomes less scarce. Machines do more. But machines require energy. So the constraint shifts.

In the automation era, the economy becomes constrained by electricity generation, grid capacity, storage, and cooling. Energy becomes central, not as an environmental debate, but as an economic reality.

Consider the scale. A single large AI datacenter can consume as much electricity as a small city, running continuously, day and night. Training a single large AI model can use electricity equivalent to hundreds of homes for a year. And training is just the beginning. Running these models in production, serving millions of users simultaneously, requires ongoing energy consumption that dwarfs the training phase.

As AI models grow larger and more numerous, energy demand scales with them. Credible estimates suggest AI could account for a significant and rapidly growing share of global electricity consumption by the end of this decade, potentially rivaling the energy consumption of major industrial nations.

If energy is cheap and abundant, automation scales faster. If energy is expensive or unstable, automation slows. Energy becomes the throttle of the future.

Energy requirements scale with automation adoption across all phases of the transition. In the near term, increases are modest as AI datacenters expand and early robotics deploy. Over the following years, demand spikes as millions of robots enter production and AI becomes infrastructure-scale. In the long term, energy becomes the binding constraint: abundant energy enables full automation abundance, while energy scarcity could force societies to choose which sectors to automate and which to leave manual. This is why energy is destiny. It determines not whether the automation era arrives, but how completely it transforms society.

The Solar Revolution

The world is already transitioning toward solar. Not because solar is fashionable, but because solar is getting cheaper. And cheap wins.

Solar has a property that makes it uniquely powerful: it's scalable. A coal plant is a giant project. A nuclear plant is a giant project. A solar farm is modular. You can build it in pieces, expand it, scale it, combine it with storage. This modularity makes solar one of the most economically aggressive technologies in history.

The cost curve has been remarkable. Over the past fifteen years, the cost of utility-scale solar has fallen by roughly 90%. In many favorable locations, solar is now the cheapest source of new electricity generation available, undercutting coal, natural gas, and in some regions even existing nuclear power.

This isn't linear improvement. It's exponential cost reduction driven by manufacturing scale, technological refinement, and supply chain optimization. The pattern resembles what happened with computer chips: the more you produce, the cheaper it gets, which enables more production, which makes it cheaper still.

And as storage improves, solar becomes more reliable. Battery costs have followed a similar decline curve, falling dramatically over the past decade. This makes round-the-clock solar-plus-storage increasingly competitive with fossil fuel plants that can run continuously.

The result: an energy world where electricity becomes cheaper, energy becomes more local, and nations become less dependent on fossil imports.

I think about this in the context of Brazil, which is blessed with extraordinary solar potential, particularly in the northeast, and already generates the majority of its electricity from hydroelectric dams. If Brazil gets the institutional and regulatory framework right, it could become one of the great energy powers of the automation era. Not through oil. Through sunlight and water. The irony would be rich: a country that spent decades trying to industrialize through cheap labor might leapfrog into the future through cheap energy.

The Geopolitical Earthquake

This has massive geopolitical consequences. Because energy dependence has fueled wars for centuries. Energy abundance changes global power.

Countries that once imported billions of dollars of fossil fuels can produce energy domestically through renewables. Oil-exporting nations face declining leverage as electricity replaces petroleum. The financial systems built around fossil fuel exports begin to weaken.

Think about what this means for economies built on oil exports. As the world electrifies and that electricity comes from domestic solar and wind rather than imported oil and gas, these nations face fundamental challenges to their economic models. Some have begun diversifying, investing sovereign wealth into technology and tourism and financial services. Others have not. The transition will be brutal for those who haven't prepared.

Meanwhile, nations with abundant renewable resources gain new advantages. Countries with geothermal energy, strong solar potential, reliable hydroelectric power, or consistent wind, these find themselves newly positioned in a global economy that increasingly values cheap electricity above cheap labor.

The energy advantage map is being redrawn.

AI Accelerates Its Own Energy Solution

Here's where it gets interesting. AI doesn't only consume energy. It accelerates energy innovation.

AI improves grid optimization, battery research, materials science, energy forecasting, and infrastructure planning. This creates a self-reinforcing loop:

AI drives energy demand. Energy demand drives investment. Investment drives innovation. Innovation drives cheaper energy. Cheaper energy drives more AI. The loop tightens. The future becomes more electrified.

The applications are already visible. AI-optimized datacenter cooling has demonstrated significant energy savings in large facilities. AI-managed grid systems reduce energy waste by improving prediction and load balancing. Machine learning accelerates materials discovery for solar panels, finding compounds with better efficiency or lower manufacturing cost. AI weather prediction improves renewable energy forecasting, allowing better grid integration.

The irony is elegant: AI's enormous energy appetite creates incentives to make energy cheaper, which enables more AI deployment, which further accelerates energy innovation.

Datacenters: The New Factories

In the industrial era, factories were the core infrastructure. In the automation era, datacenters become the factories.

Datacenters aren't "buildings with computers." They're industrial machines. They convert electricity into intelligence, prediction, automation, and economic output.

This is why the future economy will build datacenters the way the industrial era built factories. And just like factories, datacenters cluster where conditions are favorable: cheap energy, stable infrastructure, and reliable cooling.

This creates geographic specialization. Regions with geothermal power attract datacenters because they provide both cheap electricity and cold air for cooling. Areas with hydroelectric power benefit similarly. Regions with cheap wind and solar energy draw investment for the same reason.

A large datacenter represents billions of dollars in capital investment. It employs relatively few people, perhaps a few dozen to a few hundred permanent staff, but consumes as much electricity as a small city. The economic impact comes not from direct employment but from enabling digital services, AI applications, and cloud computing that power thousands of businesses.

Why Space Starts Making Economic Sense

This is where the discussion gets provocative. Because cooling is expensive. Energy location matters. Land is constrained. And the sun shines continuously in space.

Space-based solar power is an old idea. It's been discussed for decades. It was usually dismissed as too expensive, too complex, too science-fiction.

But technology changes cost curves. Launch costs are falling. Robotics is improving. Materials science is improving. Energy demand is rising. Compute demand is rising.

And once demand rises enough, previously "impossible" ideas become rational.

Space-based solar has a unique advantage: the sun shines almost continuously in orbit. No night. No clouds. No seasons. No weather. This means space-based solar can generate power with a reliability that Earth-based solar can't match.

The challenge is transmission: how do you send energy from orbit to Earth? Microwave transmission. Laser transmission. Beamed power. These sound futuristic. But incentives matter. When energy demand becomes enormous, and when launch costs continue to fall, investment follows. And investment turns futuristic concepts into engineering.

Multiple national space agencies and private companies are already investing in space-based solar research. These aren't fringe projects. They're serious engineering efforts driven by the recognition that terrestrial energy sources alone may not meet the demands of an automation-intensive economy.

The More Provocative Idea: Orbital Datacenters

Now we arrive at the more provocative idea. What if, instead of sending energy down to Earth, we move the datacenters up?

Datacenters require power, cooling, security, and real estate. Space offers abundant sunlight, natural cooling, isolation, and no land constraints.

An orbital datacenter could theoretically generate power through solar, dissipate heat through radiators, and operate without land limitations.

This sounds absurd. Until you remember something: datacenters are already built in places that seem absurd. In remote deserts. In cold northern regions. Near hydroelectric plants. One major technology company tested underwater datacenters on the ocean floor. Others operate massive facilities inside the Arctic Circle, specifically for cooling advantages.

Datacenters don't care about beauty. They care about physics. And space is the ultimate physics environment. Abundant sunlight, continuous, without atmospheric losses. Extreme cooling potential. No neighbors. No zoning boards. No land scarcity.

The economics are currently unfavorable. Launch costs would need to fall further. Radiation hardening adds expense. Maintenance requires autonomy or expensive human visits. Communication latency matters for some applications.

But the trend lines are moving. Launch costs fall. Robotics improves. Energy demand rises. Compute becomes strategic. And suddenly, space becomes plausible. Not inevitable, but plausible.

And in the automation era, plausible ideas often become real.

The Strategic Implications

If datacenters move into space, the implications are enormous. Compute becomes harder to attack, harder to regulate, harder to control. Space becomes economic territory, not only scientific territory.

This creates a new geopolitical frontier. Nations will compete for orbital slots, space infrastructure, and space energy systems.

This is why the automation era could reignite space as a strategic domain. Not because humans become romantic explorers, but because the future economy becomes compute-hungry. And compute is power.

Consider the parallels to historical infrastructure races. In the 1800s, nations competed to build railroad networks. Control over rail meant control over commerce. In the 1900s, nations competed for oil reserves. In the 2000s, fiber optic networks and undersea cables became strategic infrastructure.

Space compute could become the next equivalent: infrastructure so valuable that nations invest enormous resources to secure access and deny adversaries.

Energy Abundance as the Great Stabilizer

Now we return to Earth. Because the most important part of this chapter isn't space. It's energy abundance.

Energy abundance is one of the strongest stabilizers of civilization. Because energy scarcity has driven conflict, inflation, and inequality.

If energy becomes cheap and abundant, many costs fall: manufacturing, transportation, water desalination, food production, and housing construction. Energy abundance could reduce global suffering dramatically. Not through ideology. Through physics. Cheap energy makes everything easier.

Consider water. Desalination plants can turn seawater into fresh water, but the process is energy-intensive. Currently, desalination is expensive enough to limit its use to wealthy, water-scarce regions. But if energy costs fall substantially, desalination costs fall proportionally. Suddenly, coastal regions worldwide can afford abundant fresh water. Agricultural productivity increases. Water conflicts decrease. Hundreds of millions benefit.

Or consider food. Vertical farms can produce food year-round with minimal land and water, but they're energy-intensive: LED lighting, climate control, automation. Cheap energy makes vertical farming economical, potentially transforming food security in urban areas and harsh climates.

The Dark Side: Energy as Power Concentrator

Energy abundance can also concentrate power. If energy becomes centralized in massive infrastructure, control becomes strategic.

This is why energy policy will be one of the most important political domains of the century. Because energy isn't only economic. It's national security.

Distributed energy, rooftop solar, home batteries, microgrids, creates resilience and reduces central control. Centralized energy, massive solar farms, large nuclear plants, space-based power, creates efficiency but also creates strategic targets and control points.

The balance between distributed and centralized energy will shape both economic efficiency and political freedom in the automation era.

Energy as Destiny

The automation era will not be powered by one energy source. It'll likely be a mix: solar, wind, nuclear, storage, and grid modernization.

But the trend is clear: the future is electrified. And electricity must become cheaper, more abundant, and more reliable to support the compute-intensive economy we're building.

Energy is destiny. It determines which nations can automate fastest. Which regions can attract datacenters. Which economies can scale AI. Which societies can offer abundance to their citizens.

But energy powers more than robots and datacenters. It also powers the monetary system. Because the automation era doesn't just change how we produce things. It changes how we exchange them. How we coordinate. How money itself works.

That's what we explore next.

Chapter 12

Money at Machine Speed

Money is not a thing. It's a protocol. A social agreement. A system that coordinates trust between strangers. A system that allows the economy to function.

And the automation era forces money to evolve. Not because people suddenly become fascinated by finance, because the economy changes shape. And when the economy changes shape, the monetary system must adapt.

This is a chapter I've been wanting to write for a long time. Not just because I've spent years working in financial infrastructure at Circle, at the intersection of traditional finance and the digital systems replacing it, but because I've watched the gap between how money works today and how it will need to work tomorrow widen in real time. I've sat in meetings where billion-dollar settlement systems were discussed in the same breath as weekend banking hours. I've watched cross-border payments take days to settle while the AI systems generating those payments operated in milliseconds.

The mismatch is becoming untenable. And this chapter is about what comes next: what happens when transactions become automated, commerce becomes machine-speed, borders become less relevant to digital activity, and the economy begins to operate faster than human institutions were designed for.

The Economy Is Becoming Machine-Speed

For most of history, the economy moved at human speed. A person decided to buy something. A person decided to sell something. A person signed a contract. A person processed an invoice. A person approved a payment. A person negotiated a deal.

Even in modern finance, humans remained deeply embedded: traders, bankers, accountants, lawyers, executives, regulators.

The automation era changes this. Because AI and software agents can negotiate, optimize, transact, and settle without human involvement. The future economy won't only be automated in production, it'll be automated in coordination. And coordination is what money does.

Consider a simple example: autonomous vehicles coordinating ride-sharing. An AI system identifies that three passengers heading similar directions could share rides. It negotiates pricing, routes, and timing with each passenger's preferences. It settles payment instantly upon completion. The entire transaction, negotiation to settlement, takes seconds and involves no human approval.

Or consider automated supply chains. A factory's AI detects it's running low on a specific component. It queries suppliers, compares pricing and delivery times, negotiates terms, places an order, and arranges payment, all automatically. The transaction happens at 3 AM on a Sunday. No one is working, yet commerce continues.

This is machine-speed commerce. And it requires machine-compatible money.

The Hidden Explosion: Transaction Volume

The most underestimated effect of automation is transaction volume. When humans transact, transactions are limited by human attention. When machines transact, transactions multiply.

Machines don't get tired. They don't procrastinate. They don't sleep. They can transact continuously.

A machine economy will involve automated purchasing, automated supply chain settlement, automated insurance claims, automated micro-payments, automated subscription negotiation, automated pricing, automated taxes, and automated compliance.

Consider the volume difference. A human business might process hundreds or thousands of transactions daily. An automated system could process millions. A connected electric vehicle might microtransact for charging, tolls, parking, and services dozens of times per trip. An AI agent managing a portfolio might execute thousands of optimizations daily.

Current payment systems handle about 2,000–5,000 transactions per second globally across all major networks combined. A fully automated economy could require orders of magnitude more capacity.

The Problem with the Current System

Modern money systems are powerful, but they're not designed for machine-speed global coordination. They have friction.

Settlement delays. Banking hours. Cross-border barriers. Fees. Intermediaries. Compliance bottlenecks.

The current system was designed for a world where humans transact, banks mediate, and borders matter. The automation era pressures these assumptions. Because machines will demand instant settlement, low fees, global interoperability, and programmable rules.

Consider international wire transfers. They typically take 1–5 business days, cost $25–50, and require manual verification. For a human sending money once a month, this is tolerable. For a machine making thousands of cross-border microtransactions daily, it's unworkable.

Or consider payment reversals. Credit cards allow chargebacks up to 120 days after purchase, protecting consumers but creating uncertainty for merchants. In machine-to-machine commerce, both parties want finality. Either the payment succeeded or it didn't. Ambiguity is expensive.

The Rise of Programmable Money

The automation era introduces a simple idea: money becomes programmable. Not in a science-fiction sense, in a practical sense. Money becomes embedded in contracts, tied to conditions, automated through rules, and integrated into software systems.

This is already happening in limited ways: escrow systems, subscription billing, payment automation. But the automation era expands it dramatically.

Machines won't want to "pay invoices." They'll want to settle instantly, automatically, with minimal friction. Programmable money becomes the natural outcome.

Imagine smart contracts for insurance. Your autonomous vehicle detects a collision. Sensors verify the impact. AI assesses damage. The insurance smart contract automatically calculates payout based on pre-agreed terms. Payment settles instantly to your digital wallet. No claims adjuster. No paperwork. No waiting weeks for reimbursement.

Or imagine supply chain financing. A factory ships goods. The shipping container has IoT sensors confirming departure. A smart contract automatically releases partial payment. When sensors confirm delivery, final payment releases automatically. No invoices. No payment terms. No collections process.

CBDCs: The State's Response

When governments see money evolving, they respond. Central Bank Digital Currencies (CBDCs) are the state's attempt to modernize money while maintaining control.

CBDCs could offer faster settlement, lower transaction costs, better compliance, and more efficient distribution of social benefits. In a world where job income weakens, governments will need better tools for distributing income. CBDCs become attractive, not only as money, but as policy infrastructure.

But CBDCs also raise concerns. Because programmable state money can become surveillance money, permissioned money, and controllable money. This is why CBDCs will be controversial. Because money isn't only economic, it's freedom.

China's digital yuan provides a preview. Launched in pilot programs in 2020, it allows the government to track transactions, set expiration dates on stimulus payments (forcing spending), and potentially restrict purchases. This enables efficient policy implementation but also unprecedented surveillance.

The European Central Bank's digital euro project emphasizes privacy protections, offline payments should be anonymous like cash, they argue. But implementing true privacy while maintaining anti-money-laundering compliance creates technical tensions.

The United States has been slower to develop a CBDC, partly due to concerns about disrupting the existing banking system and partly due to political debates about government overreach. But the momentum is building as other nations advance.

Pix: A Different Kind of Monetary Innovation

Brazil offers a different model entirely. Pix, the instant payment system launched by the Central Bank of Brazil in

2020, is not a CBDC. It does not create a new currency or give the government direct control over how money is spent. What it does is eliminate friction. Pix allows any Brazilian with a bank account or digital wallet to send and receive money instantly, 24 hours a day, 7 days a week, at zero cost. Within two years of launch, it had been adopted by over 130 million people, fundamentally changing how an entire country interacts with money. Street vendors, small businesses, families splitting a dinner bill, all moved to Pix almost overnight. I watched this happen from abroad with a mix of pride and fascination, because I grew up in a country where cashing a check could take a week and transferring money between banks felt like a bureaucratic obstacle course.

Pix didn't reinvent money. It reinvented access. And it proved something important for the automation era: you don't always need a new currency to modernize a monetary system. Sometimes you just need to remove the friction from the one you already have. The lesson for other nations is that government-led monetary innovation doesn't have to mean surveillance or control. It can simply mean making existing money work the way people already expect the internet to work: instantly, freely, for everyone.

Stablecoins: The Market's Response

I need to be transparent here. I'm not a disinterested observer when it comes to stablecoins. I work at Circle, the company that issues USDC, one of the largest stablecoins in the world. That work has given me a front-row seat to something I believe is one of the most important monetary innovations of the last decade. It has also, inevitably, shaped my perspective. I'll try to be honest about both. The view expressed here are my own and do not represent those of my employer.

While governments build CBDCs, markets are already building their own monetary rails. Stablecoins are digital currencies pegged to fiat currencies like the dollar. They offer fast settlement, global transfer, internet-native interoperability, and integration with software systems.

The problem stablecoins solve isn't theoretical, it's visceral. I grew up in Brazil, a country where ordinary families have watched their savings evaporate overnight because of currency devaluation. Where people learned to distrust their own money. When I arrived at Circle and began to understand what dollar-backed stablecoins could mean for people in economies like the one I grew up in, the significance wasn't abstract to me. It was personal.

A family in São Paulo, in Lagos, in Manila, sending their children to school on remittances from a relative working abroad, loses 6–7% of every transfer to fees through traditional services. That's not a rounding error. That's meals. That's textbooks. That's medicine. Stablecoins like USDC can reduce that cost to under 1%, and settle in minutes instead of days. I've seen the numbers at scale. The human impact is real.

By 2024, stablecoins process over $10 trillion in annual transaction volume, comparable to payment processors like PayPal. Major stablecoins such as USDC and USDT settle transactions 24/7 with finality in minutes, not days. For businesses, stablecoins enable instant settlement with international partners without expensive currency conversions or multi-day waits.

But stablecoins aren't without risk or criticism. They depend on the trustworthiness and transparency of their issuers. They require regulatory clarity that is still evolving. Questions about reserve management, auditing standards, and systemic risk are legitimate and ongoing. The industry is young, and some of its early actors have not always met the standards the technology demands. Some issuers, including Circle, have emphasized transparency, with full reserve attestations, regulatory engagement, compliance-first design, but the broader ecosystem is uneven. That unevenness matters because trust, once broken, is expensive to rebuild.

What I can say from the inside is this: stablecoins are not a speculative bet on the future. They are infrastructure that is already working, already settling real value for real people, already demonstrating what machine-compatible money looks like in practice. The automation era will only accelerate that demand.

Bitcoin: The Case For and Against

Now I need to be transparent about something else.

I am a Bitcoin investor. I have been for years. I believe in Bitcoin's long-term value proposition with the kind of conviction that makes my wife occasionally roll her eyes at dinner when the conversation turns to monetary policy. I am what some people call a Bitcoin maximalist, and I'm not embarrassed by it.

But this is a book about understanding the future clearly, not about selling my portfolio. So what I owe you in this section is not persuasion, it's honesty. I'll give you the strongest case for Bitcoin in the automation era, and then I'll give you the strongest case against it. You can decide for yourself.

The Case For

The strongest argument for Bitcoin in the automation era isn't price appreciation, it's neutrality.

Bitcoin is borderless, censorship-resistant, scarce, and not controlled by any single nation. In a world where the economy becomes more global and machine-speed, neutral money becomes attractive. Because machines don't want politics in their transactions. They want finality. They want reliability. They want rules that don't change arbitrarily.

Consider the attributes machines might value. Bitcoin has a fixed supply of 21 million coins, algorithmically enforced, no central authority can print more. Transactions are irreversible once confirmed, providing settlement finality. The network operates continuously, no banking hours, no holidays. And it's permissionless: any machine can transact without approval from a government, a bank, or a compliance officer.

For international machine-to-machine commerce where trust between parties is low, Bitcoin's neutrality has appeal. Neither party can manipulate the currency. Neither party controls the settlement rails. The math is the authority.

There's also the monetary policy argument. In a world where governments may need to distribute trillions in citizens' dividends, the temptation to inflate currencies becomes enormous. Bitcoin's fixed supply acts as a hedge against that debasement. A savings technology for people and institutions that want to preserve purchasing power over decades, not just quarters.

And there's the freedom argument. In a world where CBDCs could give governments unprecedented control over how citizens spend money, Bitcoin offers an exit. Not from society, from surveillance. That matters in democracies, and it matters even more in authoritarian regimes.

This is why I hold Bitcoin. Not as a trade. As a conviction about what kind of monetary infrastructure the world will need.

The Case Against

But I would be dishonest if I pretended the case against Bitcoin doesn't exist. It does, and serious people make it.

The most practical critique is throughput. Bitcoin's base layer handles roughly 7 transactions per second. In a machine economy processing millions of microtransactions, that's comically insufficient. Yes, second-layer solutions like the Lightning Network dramatically increase capacity, enabling potentially millions of transactions per second at negligible cost by settling only the net balance on Bitcoin's base layer. But Lightning is still maturing. Its reliability, liquidity, and user experience have improved but are not yet at the level that machine-speed commerce would demand at global scale.

The volatility critique is also real. Bitcoin's price can swing 10–20% in a single week. For a store of value over decades, that volatility may wash out. But for a medium of exchange, for machines settling supply chain payments or consumers buying groceries, it's a problem. You don't want the price of your component shipment to change by 15% between when the order is placed and when it arrives. This is precisely why stablecoins exist alongside Bitcoin, they serve different functions.

The energy critique has softened as Bitcoin mining increasingly utilizes renewable and stranded energy, but it hasn't disappeared. Bitcoin's proof-of-work consensus mechanism consumes significant electricity. Comparable to a small country. Proponents argue this energy secures the network and increasingly comes from renewable sources. Critics argue the energy could be better used elsewhere, especially in an automation era that will itself be energy-hungry. Both sides have legitimate points.

The governance critique is subtle but important. Bitcoin's strength, that no one controls it, is also its limitation. Protocol upgrades are slow and contentious. Adapting to new requirements takes years of community consensus. In a machine economy that evolves rapidly, a monetary system that changes slowly may find itself outpaced by more agile alternatives.

And finally, there's the adoption question. Bitcoin has been around since 2009. It has achieved significant recognition as a store of value and has been adopted as legal tender in El Salvador. But it has not yet become a widely used medium of exchange for everyday commerce. Whether it will, or whether it will remain primarily "digital gold" while other systems handle daily transactions, is a genuinely open question.

Where I Land

I'll tell you where I land, and you can weight my bias accordingly.

I believe Bitcoin will play a significant role in the monetary architecture of the automation era, primarily as a neutral reserve asset, a hedge against currency debasement, and a censorship-resistant alternative for people and machines that need financial sovereignty. I don't believe it will replace the dollar, or stablecoins, or CBDCs for everyday transactions. It doesn't need to. Gold didn't process grocery payments either, and it anchored the global monetary system for centuries.

But I hold this view with humility. The monetary future is not written. Bitcoin could become everything its believers hope for, or it could be outcompeted by systems that don't yet exist. What I'm confident about is that the automation era will demand monetary innovation, and Bitcoin, whatever its ultimate role, is the most important experiment in that innovation since Bretton Woods.

The Monetary Ecosystem

The future monetary system won't be one currency. It'll be an ecosystem. Different forms of money will serve different roles:

CBDCs for domestic policy and distribution. Stablecoins for commerce and settlement. Bitcoin for neutral reserve and censorship-resistant value storage. Traditional banking for credit and legacy infrastructure.

The automation era doesn't eliminate old systems overnight. It layers new systems on top. And over time, the new systems become normal. Then invisible.

I've seen this layering happen firsthand at Circle. When USDC first launched, skeptics dismissed it as a niche tool for crypto traders. Within a few years, it was being used by businesses for cross-border payments, by NGOs for aid distribution, by individuals in unstable economies as a savings vehicle. The transition from "crypto curiosity" to "serious financial infrastructure" happened faster than almost anyone predicted. The same layering will occur across the entire monetary ecosystem as the automation era accelerates demand.

The End of Borders for Money

One of the most profound effects of digital money is this: borders become less relevant. Not politically, economically.

Digital money moves globally, instantly. And when money moves globally, the economy becomes more fluid. Capital flows faster. Commerce becomes more global. Work becomes more distributed.

And governments face a new challenge: How do you regulate money that moves like information?

This is one of the great governance challenges of the automation era. Because money isn't only an economic tool, it's a power tool.

Nations historically controlled money through central banks, banking regulations, capital controls, and currency monopolies. But digital money that operates peer-to-peer, crosses borders instantly, and settles without intermediaries challenges all these control mechanisms.

The Automation Era's Money Problem

The automation era introduces a new money problem. Not inflation. Not interest rates. Distribution.

If job income weakens, governments must distribute income differently. This requires efficient rails, low friction, and scalable systems. Digital money becomes essential, because you can't distribute social income efficiently through slow, expensive banking systems.

Consider universal basic income distribution. If a government provides $1,000 monthly to 200 million citizens, that's 200 million transactions monthly. Traditional banking infrastructure handles this slowly and expensively: paper checks, account processing, fraud prevention.

A CBDC or stablecoins could distribute payments instantly to digital wallets at negligible cost. Recipients access funds immediately. Administrative overhead drops dramatically. This efficiency makes policies like UBI more feasible.

The Political Battle Over Money

Money will become one of the most politically contested domains of the automation era. Because digital money can be designed for freedom or control.

The same tools that allow efficient distribution can also allow surveillance. The same systems that allow instant settlement can also allow censorship.

This is why the monetary system isn't only technical, it's philosophical. It forces societies to ask: Do we want money that's programmable by the state? Or money that's neutral and unstoppable? Or some mixture of both?

The answer will vary by country. And that variation will shape global power.

Authoritarian regimes may favor CBDCs with extensive surveillance and control features. Democracies may balance efficiency with privacy protections. Some populations may embrace neutral, decentralized alternatives like Bitcoin as protection against government overreach.

Having worked in both traditional finance and at the frontier of digital money, I can tell you that these aren't theoretical debates. They're happening right now, in regulatory conversations, in product design meetings, in legislative drafts. The decisions being made today about monetary architecture will shape individual freedom and government power for decades. The automation era simply raises the stakes, because when income flows through digital systems by necessity, whoever controls those systems controls far more than money.

The monetary architecture societies choose will reflect their values, and shape their futures.

Beyond Money: The Knowledge Revolution

Money is how we coordinate economic activity. But there's another system that shapes human potential even more fundamentally: education. How we learn. How we develop capability. How knowledge is transmitted across generations.

And just as automation transforms money into something machine-compatible, it transforms education into something democratically accessible in ways that were never before possible.

That revolution, and its consequences, is what we explore next.

Chapter 13
The Education Revolution

Of all the transformations the automation era will bring, one stands out as the most hopeful: education becomes democratically accessible in ways that were never before possible.

Education is how civilizations transmit knowledge across generations. It's how children become citizens. How talent becomes capability. How potential becomes contribution.

But education has always been constrained by scarcity. Not scarcity of information. Scarcity of teaching.

A great teacher can only teach so many students. A tutor is expensive. A mentor is rare. A classroom is limited. A school is limited. Education, at its core, has been a system for distributing human attention. And human attention is scarce.

The automation era changes this. Because AI tutors collapse the scarcity of teaching. And when teaching becomes scalable, education becomes abundant.

This is personal for me. I came from a good family in Brazil, and I had access to decent schools and eventually to international education. But I watched classmates who were just as smart, just as curious, just as capable, fall behind because the system couldn't give them what they needed. A kid who struggled with math didn't get a tutor. They got left behind. A kid who learned faster than the class didn't get challenged. They got bored. The bottleneck was never talent. It was always attention. Human attention, distributed unevenly and scarce by nature.

This is one of the most hopeful possibilities of the entire century. But it also introduces one of the most difficult challenges: when knowledge becomes free, what happens to motivation?

The Great Misunderstanding About Education

Most people think education is about information. It isn't.

Information has been abundant for decades. The internet already contains more knowledge than any library in history. Video platforms have tutorials on every conceivable skill. Free online encyclopedias have more articles than any printed encyclopedia ever did. Open courseware from major universities covers nearly every academic subject.

Yet educational inequality persists. Why?

Because education isn't primarily about access to information. It's about explanation, feedback, repetition, encouragement, and structure.

A student doesn't fail because the information is missing. A student fails because they don't understand, they don't get feedback, they don't have support, and they don't have a personalized path.

This is why tutoring is so powerful. A tutor adapts. A tutor explains differently. A tutor notices confusion. A tutor builds confidence.

Tutoring has always been one of the most effective forms of education. Research consistently shows that one-on-one tutoring produces dramatic improvements in learning outcomes, often transforming average students into top performers. It's also been one of the most expensive. For a family earning median income, sustained tutoring is financially impossible.

AI tutors change this.

The AI Tutor: A Civilizational Upgrade

An AI tutor can explain concepts in multiple ways, adapt to the student's pace, provide endless practice, identify weaknesses, and respond without frustration.

A human tutor might be available for one hour a week. An AI tutor is available all day. For millions.

This isn't a small change. It's a civilizational upgrade. Because education is one of the strongest levers for human potential. If education becomes more personalized and accessible, the floor rises. And when the floor rises, society becomes more capable.

Early AI tutoring systems are already showing remarkable results. Students using AI-powered math tutors have shown substantial improvement compared to traditional instruction. Language learning with AI conversation partners accelerates fluency acquisition significantly compared to classroom-only instruction. These are early results, and they'll improve as the technology matures.

Consider a concrete scenario. A twelve-year-old struggling with algebra has a tired teacher managing thirty students. The teacher has forty-five minutes. If the student gets confused, they might receive five minutes of individual attention, not enough to truly grasp the concept.

With an AI tutor, this child can ask the same question fifteen different ways. The AI patiently explains, generates practice problems at exactly the right difficulty, identifies which prerequisite concept is missing, and works through examples until understanding clicks. At 10 PM when homework frustration peaks, the AI is still there. No judgment. No fatigue. Infinite patience.

This is the automation era's greatest educational gift: making world-class tutoring available to everyone.

The Democratization of Elite Learning

For most of history, elite education was scarce. Not because knowledge was secret. Because teaching was scarce.

The best teachers were rare. The best schools were limited. The best mentorship was concentrated in wealthy institutions. If you attended one of the world's top universities, you had access to extraordinary professors, brilliant peers, extensive libraries, and rich intellectual communities. If you attended an underfunded rural school, you had overcrowded classrooms, outdated textbooks, and overwhelmed teachers.

AI tutors democratize elite learning. A student in a poor region could access world-class explanations, personalized practice, and adaptive learning pathways.

This is the kind of change that could reduce global inequality. Not by redistributing money, but by redistributing capability.

A brilliant child born in rural India or sub-Saharan Africa, who historically would have had limited educational access, could learn mathematics from AI systems trained on insights from the world's best mathematicians. Could learn programming from tutorials explaining concepts as clearly as top-tier professors. Could learn science with simulations and visualizations that would have cost millions to produce.

I think about what this would have meant growing up in Porto Alegre. I was fortunate. My family sent me to a good private school, and I had access to solid teachers and resources. But I had friends from public schools across the city who were just as sharp, just as hungry to learn, and who got a fraction of the attention. The difference between us wasn't talent. It was which side of a tuition payment you landed on. AI tutoring doesn't solve every structural barrier. But it breaks the most fundamental one: the scarcity of excellent teaching.

The democratization isn't complete or automatic. Infrastructure, motivation, and support still matter. But the constraint shifts from scarcity of teachers to availability of basic internet access.

The New Literacy: Self-Direction

Now we arrive at the paradox. If AI tutors make learning easier, why is there a problem?

Because education isn't only about learning. It's about motivation.

The industrial era made education functional. Education was tied to jobs. You studied to get credentials. You got credentials to get employment. Employment provided income. Income provided survival. This created a motivation engine. Even if learning was boring, it was necessary.

The automation era weakens the link between education and jobs. If jobs weaken, the motivation engine weakens. So the automation era demands a new skill: self-direction.

Self-direction is the ability to set goals, pursue mastery, maintain discipline, and build meaning without external coercion. In the old world, survival coerced discipline. In the new world, freedom requires discipline.

This is one of the most important psychological shifts of the century.

Consider the difference. A college student in the 20th century studied calculus because it was required for an engineering degree, which led to employment, which enabled survival. The motivation was clear and external.

A person in the automation era might have basic income and abundant free time. They could learn calculus for intellectual satisfaction, creative problem-solving, or personal growth. But the motivation must be internal. No one is forcing them. No survival benefit compels them.

Some people thrive with this freedom. They become polymath learners, exploring mathematics, philosophy, art, and science driven by curiosity. Others drift, lacking the structure that external pressure provided.

Schools Will Not Disappear

A common prediction is that AI will replace schools. This is unlikely.

Because schools aren't only information delivery systems. Schools are social environments, community centers, discipline structures, and identity systems.

Children don't only learn math in school. They learn cooperation, conflict resolution, friendship, social hierarchy, and belonging. AI can't replace that.

What AI will replace is the scarcity model of teaching. The role of the teacher shifts from information delivery to mentorship, coaching, and human development. Teachers become more like guides, mentors, and culture-builders.

This is a profound upgrade. Because one of the tragedies of modern education is that teachers spend too much time on bureaucracy and repetition. Grading hundreds of worksheets. Repeating explanations for the fifth time. Managing administrative tasks. Dealing with standardized test preparation.

AI can remove that friction. Let AI grade assignments, generate practice problems, provide explanations, and track progress. Free teachers to do what humans do best: inspire, encourage, mentor, and build relationships.

Imagine a classroom where the teacher knows exactly which students are struggling with which concepts because AI has tracked their work and flagged patterns. The teacher spends time with struggling students one-on-one, providing encouragement and context. Meanwhile, advanced students work on challenging projects with AI assistance, moving at their own pace.

This is education becoming more human, not less.

The Collapse of Credential Monopolies

Education has another function: credentials. Degrees. Certificates. Signals.

Credentials exist because employers need a way to filter talent. Degrees became a proxy for capability. Not perfectly, but functionally.

AI changes this. Because AI makes learning cheaper. And because AI also makes assessment easier. Skill-based hiring may rise: portfolios, demonstrations, projects, competency tests.

Credentials won't vanish. But their monopoly weakens.

This is disruptive. Because universities aren't only education systems. They're status systems, economic systems, identity systems. The automation era challenges them.

Consider software engineering. Traditionally, you needed a computer science degree to be hired at a serious company.

Now, self-taught programmers and bootcamp graduates with strong project portfolios routinely get hired at competitive salaries. Employers care more about demonstrated ability. Can you actually build things? That matters more than where you studied.

This pattern could expand across professions. A graphic designer showcases their portfolio. A writer shares published work. A data scientist demonstrates projects analyzing real datasets. Direct evidence of capability matters more than degrees.

But this also creates challenges. How do you verify capabilities without credible institutions? How do you prevent fraud? Who defines standards? These questions remain unsolved.

The Future of Universities

Universities will face a choice. They can remain credential factories or they can become human development institutions.

The universities that thrive will likely focus on mentorship, research, community, and identity. They'll become less about lectures and more about networks, projects, and belonging.

Because lectures are the easiest thing for AI to replicate. The human value of a university isn't the lecture. It's the environment. The culture. The peer group. The mentorship. The social ecosystem.

The value of an elite university has never been purely academic. It's the network, the signal, the community, the resources, the identity. Being a graduate of a top institution opens doors not because you necessarily learned more, you could learn similar content elsewhere, but because of what that credential signals and the relationships it creates.

Elite universities will likely remain valuable for these network effects. But mid-tier universities whose primary value was information delivery and basic credentialing face pressure.

Education must teach ladder-building, not just ladder-climbing. How to create opportunity when traditional pathways break.

The Risk: A Motivation Crisis

Now we reach the danger. If education becomes easy and accessible, why wouldn't everyone keep learning?

Because learning is hard. Not intellectually. Emotionally. Learning requires discomfort, failure, repetition, and patience.

In the old world, the reward was survival. In the new world, the reward is meaning. And meaning is harder to grasp than survival.

This is why the automation era risks creating a motivation crisis. A society where knowledge is abundant, but discipline is scarce, and purpose is unclear. This is one of the deepest challenges of the post-work world.

Research on sudden freedom from structure, whether through early retirement, inheritance, or other windfalls, reveals a consistent pattern: many people drift rather than flourish. Without external demands, creating meaningful routines becomes psychologically demanding. Depression rates increase. Satisfaction decreases.

The automation era risks creating this psychology at scale: populations with abundant resources and knowledge but lacking clear purpose.

The Great Opportunity: A Renaissance of Mastery

Now we return to hope. Because the automation era also offers something extraordinary.

If people are freed from survival labor, they can pursue mastery. Not as a luxury, but as a human calling. The future could produce more artists, more scientists, more builders, more philosophers, more caregivers, more explorers, more community leaders.

Not because society becomes utopian, but because time becomes available. And tools become powerful. AI can act as a mentor, a collaborator, a guide, a teacher. This could unlock human creativity at a scale never seen.

The automation era could become a renaissance. But only if purpose is cultivated.

Consider historical precedents. The Renaissance flourished partly because wealthy patrons freed artists and thinkers from survival concerns. Michelangelo could spend years on the Sistine Chapel. Da Vinci could pursue diverse interests across art, engineering, and science. The automation era could democratize this pattern. Instead of a few dozen patronized geniuses, imagine millions of people pursuing deep work in their chosen domains, supported by basic income, empowered by AI tools, freed from survival labor.

I think about Luca when I imagine this future. He's sixteen, and he has curiosities that don't fit neatly into any curriculum. He's passionate about movies and music, follows politics with an intensity that surprises me, and plans to pursue a career in medicine. The industrial education system would funnel him into a pre-med track and tell him the rest is extracurricular. The automation era might let him build something more interesting: a doctor who understands the political systems that shape public health, who brings a storyteller's eye to patient care, who never had to abandon his broader curiosities to survive organic chemistry. AI tools don't replace the hard work of medical training. But they make the learning curve less punishing and the path less narrow.

The Education System Must Teach Purpose

This is the key. In the automation era, education can't only teach knowledge. It must teach self-direction, discipline, meaning-making, and contribution.

The future education system must answer a new question: what does it mean to be a human in a world where survival doesn't require work?

That's not a technical question. It's a cultural question. And it's one of the reasons the automation era is so profound.

Because it forces civilization to redefine adulthood. In the old world, adulthood meant earning. In the new world, adulthood may mean choosing.

Choosing purpose. Choosing contribution. Choosing mastery. Choosing service.

This is harder. And also more beautiful.

The Question That Follows

Education is one of the most hopeful domains of the automation era. But it leads directly to the most difficult.

Because once people have time, stability, and knowledge, they face the most human question of all: what is my life for?

The automation era doesn't only change the economy. It changes identity. It changes motivation. It changes meaning.

This is the purpose problem. And it's the deepest challenge of abundance. That's what we explore next.

Chapter 14

The Purpose Problem

There's a strange thing about human beings.

We can endure hardship. We can endure struggle. We can endure poverty. We can endure pain. We can endure war. We can endure scarcity. History is proof. Humans are resilient creatures.

But there's something humans struggle with far more than hardship. Something that breaks people quietly. Not through violence. Through emptiness.

Humans struggle with meaninglessness.

This is the central psychological challenge of the automation era. Not unemployment. Not even inequality. Purpose.

Because the automation era does something no previous era has done at scale: it loosens the link between survival and labor. And when survival no longer requires work, work stops being the default source of meaning.

That sounds liberating. And it is. But it's also destabilizing. Because modern civilization has built an entire identity system around work. Remove work, and you remove the scaffolding. And once the scaffolding is gone, many people face a terrifying question: who am I without my job?

I've asked myself this question. Not because I've lost a job, but because I've watched the meaning of my own work shift underneath me. I came into finance because I liked building things, solving problems, creating value. As AI tools have become more capable, I've watched tasks that used to require my judgment get handled by systems that are faster and, in some narrow domains, more reliable. The honest version of my reaction wasn't fear of unemployment. It was something subtler: a recalibration of where my value actually lives. If the analytical work is automated, what's left? Relationships. Judgment in ambiguous situations. The ability to ask the right questions rather than compute the right answers. But even naming those things required a kind of self-examination that most people never have to do when the old structures are intact.

Work Was Never Only About Money

We must begin with honesty. Work was never only about income.

Work gave structure, routine, identity, status, community, and a sense of contribution. Work gave people a reason to wake up. A sense of progress. A sense of being needed. A sense of belonging.

Work was the default meaning system of modern society. Even if people hated their jobs. Even if work was stressful. Even if work was unfair. It still provided structure. And structure matters.

Studies of unemployment consistently show this. The financial stress is real and significant. But the psychological damage extends far beyond money. Unemployed workers report feeling worthless, invisible, ashamed. Depression rates increase substantially. Suicide risk rises. Marriages strain. Social networks erode.

And this happens even when unemployment benefits provide adequate income. Money helps, but it doesn't solve the identity crisis. Because work provided more than a paycheck. It provided daily routine, somewhere to be, tasks to complete. It provided social connection, coworkers, professional networks, shared purpose. It provided status and respect, job titles, career progression, professional identity. And it provided meaning, contribution to something larger than oneself.

The automation era weakens work's universality. Not because work disappears, but because work becomes less necessary. And when work becomes less necessary, the meaning system weakens.

The Hidden Role of Scarcity

Scarcity forces purpose. In a scarce world, you don't need to ask: "What is my purpose?"

You need to survive. You need to provide. You need to endure.

Scarcity creates automatic meaning. Not deep meaning, but functional meaning.

The automation era reduces scarcity. It reduces survival pressure. This is good. But it also removes automatic structure.

So the automation era creates a new challenge: meaning must become self-generated. And self-generated meaning is harder than survival. Because survival is external. Meaning is internal.

Consider Viktor Frankl's observations in concentration camps. He noticed that prisoners who maintained a sense of purpose, however small, survived longer than those who lost meaning. Purpose sustained people through unimaginable hardship.

But abundance creates the opposite challenge: how do you generate purpose when survival is secured?

This isn't theoretical. Research on sudden freedom from financial pressure, whether through windfalls, early retirement, or inheritance, reveals consistent patterns. Depression, substance abuse, relationship breakdown, and loss of direction. Without external structure, many people struggle to create internal purpose.

The Comfort Trap

The automation era will likely create a world of increasing comfort. Not perfectly. Not evenly. But broadly.

Goods become cheaper. Services become cheaper. Transportation becomes easier. Entertainment becomes endless. Time becomes more available.

This is the comfort trap. Because comfort is not fulfillment. Comfort is pleasant. But fulfillment requires struggle. Humans need challenge. We need growth. We need mastery. We need contribution. A life of endless comfort becomes stagnant. And stagnation becomes depression.

Research on happiness consistently shows this pattern. Above a certain income threshold, additional money provides diminishing returns on life satisfaction. But challenge, growth, mastery, and contribution continue mattering at all income levels.

Some of the most materially comfortable societies on Earth also report significant rates of antidepressant use and mental health challenges. Comfort alone doesn't guarantee wellbeing.

The New Addiction: Infinite Distraction

The easiest way to avoid the purpose question is distraction. Modern civilization already offers distraction at scale: social media, streaming, gaming, endless content.

The automation era makes distraction more powerful. AI will personalize entertainment. Algorithms will optimize attention capture. Virtual worlds will become immersive. Content will become infinite.

A society with more free time and more powerful distraction risks becoming a society of passive consumption. And passive consumption is not meaning. It's sedation.

This is one of the most dangerous risks of abundance. Not hunger. Not poverty. But the slow erosion of ambition.

We already see early versions of this. People in developed countries spend a remarkable portion of their waking hours on screens. Research increasingly links excessive screen time to anxiety, depression, loneliness, and decreased life satisfaction. Yet screen time continues increasing.

The automation era amplifies this risk. When AI can generate perfectly personalized content, entertainment that knows exactly what holds your attention, the pull toward passive consumption intensifies. When virtual worlds offer more stimulation than physical reality, when algorithms optimize for engagement rather than wellbeing, populations risk drifting into comfortable numbness.

I notice this pull in myself. After a long day, the easiest thing is to scroll, to watch, to consume. The harder thing is to create, to build, to engage with something that pushes back. The automation era will make the easy path easier and the hard path more optional. That's a dangerous combination.

The Status Problem

Purpose isn't only internal. It's social. Humans are status creatures. We care about respect, recognition, and belonging.

Work provided status: titles, careers, prestige. The automation era destabilizes status systems. If fewer people work, what becomes prestigious? If income is distributed through citizenship, what becomes admirable?

Societies will need new status systems. Because status doesn't disappear. It simply relocates.

The risk is that status becomes tied to wealth ownership, social influence, or artificial metrics. This could intensify inequality. Not only economic. Social. A society where status is concentrated becomes culturally unstable. Because humans need dignity. And dignity requires recognition.

Consider social media's status economy. Followers, engagement, views. These become proxy measures of worth. But they're hollow metrics, disconnected from genuine contribution. The automation era risks extending this pattern: status becomes about visibility, influence, or inherited wealth rather than meaningful contribution.

The Dignity Problem

The purpose problem is also the dignity problem. A society can provide income and still create humiliation. A society can provide stability and still create emptiness.

The automation era must build dignity systems. It must honor contribution beyond employment: caregiving, mentorship, community building, art, service, mastery.

These must be socially legitimate. Not treated as hobbies. Not treated as laziness. This is one of the most important cultural redesigns of the century. Because without dignity, income becomes charity. And charity breeds resentment.

The future must not be designed as: "Here is money because you are unnecessary." It must be designed as: "Here is stability because you are a citizen in a society of abundance, and your contribution matters in many forms."

This framing matters. Because humans don't only need resources. We need respect.

Consider someone who spends thirty hours weekly caring for an aging parent with dementia. This is exhausting, skilled, emotionally demanding work. Yet it provides no income, no career progression, no professional status. In our current system, caregiving is economically invisible despite being socially essential. Or consider someone who coaches youth sports, mentors struggling students, organizes community gardens, or leads neighborhood projects. These contributions create enormous social value but no formal recognition. The automation era could redefine contribution to honor these activities. Not as hobbies, but as legitimate forms of social participation deserving respect.

My mom spent years caring for family members, managing households, building the kind of social fabric that holds communities together. None of it appeared on a resume. None of it earned a title. But without that work, everything else would have collapsed. The automation era gives us an opportunity to finally recognize that kind of contribution as what it is: essential.

The Purpose Renaissance

Now we arrive at the hopeful possibility. The automation era could produce a renaissance of purpose.

Because when humans are freed from survival labor, they can pursue mastery, service, creation, exploration, family, and community. This is the dream. Not endless leisure. Meaningful freedom.

A society where people choose work because it's fulfilling, not because it's required. This is one of the most radical possibilities in human history.

History offers glimpses. The Renaissance flourished partly because wealthy patrons freed artists from survival concerns. Athens' golden age happened when leisure enabled philosophy and politics. The post-war economic boom enabled broader educational access, producing scientific and cultural advances.

The automation era could democratize this pattern at unprecedented scale.

The Three Pillars of Purpose

In a post-work society, purpose will likely come from three pillars:

Mastery. The pursuit of skill, craft, excellence. This is deeply human. Humans are designed to improve, to build, to learn. Mastery creates meaning because it creates growth. Consider hobbyists who spend years perfecting woodworking, learning languages, or mastering musical instruments. Not for income, but for the intrinsic satisfaction of excellence. The automation era could make this universal rather than exceptional.

Service. Contribution to others: caregiving, mentorship, community. Humans are social creatures. We find meaning in helping. Research consistently shows that volunteering increases happiness and life satisfaction. People who regularly help others report better mental health, stronger sense of purpose, and greater life meaning.

Belonging. Community, family, tribe, shared identity. Humans are not designed to be isolated. The automation era risks isolation. But it can also enable deeper community if designed well.

These pillars aren't new. They're ancient. The difference is that, in the automation era, they become central. Because survival labor no longer dominates life.

The Redesign of Adulthood

This is one of the most profound shifts. In the industrial era, adulthood meant earning. In the automation era, adulthood may mean choosing.

Choosing purpose. Choosing contribution. Choosing mastery. Choosing service.

This is harder. Because the old world gave people a script: go to school, get a job, work, retire. The new world may not. The new world may require people to design their own lives. And designing your own life is a skill. It's not automatic.

This is why the automation era will require a new form of education. Not only knowledge, but life design, meaning-making, self-direction.

The Risk: A Two-Class Purpose Society

One of the darkest possibilities is that purpose becomes a luxury.

The wealthy and secure class may have time, resources, and

cultural permission to pursue meaningful lives. The insecure class may experience instability, humiliation, and drift.

This would create not only economic inequality, but existential inequality. A society where some people flourish and others rot. This is not stable. And it's not inevitable. But it's a risk.

The solution is cultural and institutional. Purpose must be democratized. Not as forced meaning, but as supported meaning.

The Role of Institutions

Institutions will matter more than ever. Because institutions shape community, identity, and contribution.

In the industrial era, jobs were institutions. They provided routine, social networks, and identity. If jobs weaken, new institutions must fill the gap.

Community organizations. Learning guilds. Service networks. Cultural groups. Sports. Arts. Local projects. Mentorship programs. The automation era will require a reinvention of community. Otherwise, loneliness becomes the epidemic of abundance.

Examples exist. Maker spaces where people collaboratively build projects. Community gardens where neighbors grow food together. Open-source communities where people contribute to shared projects. Running clubs, book clubs, mutual aid networks. These provide structure, belonging, and purpose outside employment.

The challenge is scaling these models. Making them accessible. Providing resources and recognition.

The Purpose Problem Is the Real Test

Most futurists focus on technology. But the real test of the automation era isn't technical. It's human.

Can we build a society where abundance doesn't create emptiness, freedom doesn't create drift, and stability doesn't create stagnation?

This is the purpose problem. And it will define whether the automation era becomes a renaissance or a crisis.

When Life Becomes Longer

Purpose is the deepest human challenge of abundance. But abundance also changes biology.

Because AI won't only reshape work. It'll reshape medicine. It'll accelerate drug discovery. It'll improve diagnostics. It'll extend healthspan. It'll extend life expectancy.

And when life becomes longer, the purpose problem becomes even more important. Because a longer life requires meaning that lasts.

The automation era isn't only about jobs. It's about life itself. That's what we explore next.

Chapter 15
The Longevity Revolution

If the automation era only changed work, it would already be one of the greatest transformations in human history.

But the automation era isn't only an economic revolution. It's also a biological revolution.

Because artificial intelligence won't only reshape industries. It'll reshape medicine. It'll accelerate discovery. It'll improve diagnostics. It'll personalize treatment. It'll extend healthspan.

And it may extend life expectancy in ways that feel almost surreal.

This chapter is about the second great revolution inside the automation era: longer, healthier lives. Less suffering. More prevention. More years of vitality. And a profound reshaping of what it means to be human.

Because when life becomes longer, everything changes. Retirement changes. Family structure changes. Career structure changes. Education changes. Identity changes. And purpose becomes even more central.

I should disclose something before we go further. I'm not a scientist or a physician. My understanding of medicine comes from reading, from conversations with people who work in healthcare and biotech, and from the deeply personal experience of watching people I love age, get sick, and sometimes not get better. My father is in his seventies in Garopaba, healthy and active, but I'm old enough now to notice the trajectory. The gap between his energy today and his energy five years ago is visible. The longevity revolution isn't an abstraction for me. It's the difference between how many good years my father has left, how many years I have with my children as an active, present parent, and whether my generation ages the way our parents did or differently.

Why Medicine Was Always Slow

Medicine has always been constrained by complexity. The human body isn't a machine. It's a dynamic system. Billions of cells. Thousands of pathways. Feedback loops. Interactions. Emergent behavior.

For centuries, medicine advanced slowly because experimentation is expensive, human trials are slow, data is messy, and biology is complex.

Drug discovery takes years. Clinical trials take years. Regulatory approval takes years. And many diseases remain poorly understood.

The traditional drug development timeline is staggering. From initial discovery to market approval typically takes a decade or more. The cost runs into the billions. The vast majority of candidate drugs fail somewhere along the way. Only a small fraction of drugs entering clinical trials eventually reach patients.

This slow pace has been the constraint on medical progress. Not lack of intelligence. Not lack of effort. Complexity and time.

AI changes this. Not overnight, but meaningfully.

AI as Medical Pattern Recognition

AI's greatest strength in medicine isn't replacing doctors. It's detecting patterns humans can't see.

A human doctor can analyze dozens of data points. AI can analyze millions. A radiologist can examine hundreds of scans in a career. AI can examine hundreds of thousands in hours.

This isn't about replacing human judgment. It's about augmenting detection. AI sees patterns earlier. It notices anomalies. It predicts risk. It provides decision support.

This shifts medicine from reactive to proactive. And proactive medicine is the key to longevity.

The real-world applications are already emerging. AI systems analyzing retinal scans can predict cardiovascular disease risk with surprising accuracy, detecting patterns invisible to human ophthalmologists. AI analyzing voice patterns can detect early signs of neurological disease years before traditional diagnosis. Machine learning models examining genetic data can identify cancer risk profiles and suggest preventive interventions.

In radiology, AI systems now match or exceed human radiologists at detecting certain cancers in imaging scans. This isn't replacing radiologists. It's giving them powerful tools to catch what they might miss, reducing false negatives and saving lives.

The Preventive Revolution

The greatest healthcare savings in history won't come from cheaper surgery. They'll come from prevention.

Prevention is the cheapest medicine. The most humane medicine. The most effective medicine.

AI accelerates prevention because it can detect early signals, predict risk trajectories, and personalize interventions.

Imagine a world where cancer is detected years earlier, heart disease is predicted before symptoms appear, diabetes risk is managed proactively, and mental health is supported continuously. This isn't fantasy. This is the direction of AI medicine. It'll arrive unevenly. But it'll arrive. And it'll change life expectancy.

Consider the economics. Treating late-stage cancer costs hundreds of thousands of dollars and often fails. Detecting cancer early through AI-enhanced screening costs relatively little and has dramatically better outcomes. Early-stage breast cancer has survival rates above 95%. Late-stage drops precipitously. The same pattern holds for virtually every major disease: earlier detection means better outcomes at lower cost.

Or consider diabetes. Managing diabetes with complications is enormously expensive. Preventing diabetes through early lifestyle intervention costs a fraction of that. AI systems analyzing continuous glucose monitors, activity trackers, and diet logs can predict diabetes risk years in advance and suggest personalized prevention strategies.

Cardiovascular disease remains the leading cause of death globally. But many of these deaths are preventable. AI systems analyzing wearable data, genetic profiles, and lifestyle factors can identify high-risk individuals and enable targeted interventions, medication, lifestyle changes, closer monitoring, before heart attacks or strokes occur.

The End of One-Size-Fits-All Medicine

Modern medicine is often statistical. A drug works for the average patient. A treatment is designed for population-level outcomes.

But humans aren't average. Genetics differ. Metabolism differs. Lifestyle differs. Environment differs.

AI enables personalized medicine. Treatment becomes tailored. Dosages become optimized. Side effects become predicted. Drug interactions become managed. This improves outcomes and reduces suffering.

Consider cancer treatment. Traditional chemotherapy uses standardized protocols. Same drugs, same doses for patients with similar cancer types. But patients respond differently due to genetic variations in how they metabolize drugs or how their tumors behave.

AI-driven personalized oncology analyzes tumor genetics, patient genetics, and treatment response data from thousands of similar cases, then predicts which treatments will work best for this specific patient. This increases treatment effectiveness while reducing unnecessary suffering from treatments unlikely to work.

Or consider psychiatric medication. Finding the right antidepressant is often trial-and-error. Trying one drug for months, then switching if it doesn't work. AI systems analyzing genetic markers, brain imaging, and symptom patterns can predict which medications will work for which patients, reducing the months or years of suffering through ineffective treatments.

Drug Discovery at Machine Speed

Drug discovery is one of the most expensive and slow processes in modern science. AI accelerates it by simulating molecules, predicting protein structures, exploring chemical space, and identifying promising candidates faster.

This compresses timelines. It reduces cost. It increases the number of experiments possible. AI turns drug discovery from a slow craft into a high-throughput search.

This doesn't eliminate the need for human trials, but it accelerates the pipeline. And acceleration saves lives.

The most dramatic example so far involves AI systems that can predict how proteins fold, a problem that had stymied structural biology for decades. Determining a single protein's structure experimentally could take months or years. AI systems now predict protein structures in hours with accuracy comparable to experimental methods. In a matter of months, AI generated a database of predicted structures for over two hundred million proteins, more than humanity had determined experimentally in fifty years of research. Researchers worldwide now use these predictions to design new drugs, understand disease mechanisms, and develop treatments.

AI-driven drug design is also showing promise. Rather than having human chemists design molecules one at a time based on intuition and experience, AI systems can generate thousands of candidate compounds computationally, simulate their properties, and identify the most promising ones before a single molecule is synthesized in a lab. Early results from several biotech companies suggest this approach can compress the preclinical discovery phase from years to months, and reduce costs by an order of magnitude.

Multiple AI-designed drug candidates are already in clinical trials as of this writing. These are actual molecules, designed or identified by AI systems, being tested in humans. Some target diseases that have resisted traditional approaches. Others address rare conditions that were previously uneconomical to pursue because the patient populations were too small to justify billions in development costs.

If the early results hold, the implications are profound. Drug development could become substantially faster and cheaper. More diseases could be treated. Rare conditions could become economically viable targets. Personalized treatments designed for specific tumor genetics or individual patient profiles could move from research curiosity to clinical reality.

This is one of the clearest examples of AI creating value that simply didn't exist before. Not by replacing human scientists, but by augmenting them. By letting them explore chemical space that was previously impossible to search efficiently. By compressing decades of work into years.

The longevity revolution isn't only about detecting disease earlier or personalizing treatment. It's also about discovering treatments faster. And AI is proving it can do exactly that.

The Longevity Target: Healthspan

When people talk about longevity, they often imagine living longer. But living longer isn't the goal. Living better is.

The true target is healthspan: the number of years you live in good health. Years of vitality. Years of independence. Years of clarity. Years without chronic suffering.

AI will likely extend healthspan first. Not by adding decades overnight, but by reducing disease burden. By improving prevention. By optimizing treatment.

This is a massive upgrade. Because the greatest tragedy of modern medicine isn't death. It's prolonged decline. Longevity medicine aims to compress decline. To extend vitality. To reduce suffering.

Consider current reality. In most developed countries, there's a significant gap between life expectancy and healthy life expectancy. People live into their seventies and beyond, but the last decade or more is often marked by chronic disease, declining independence, and diminished quality of life. The gap between total years lived and years lived well can be a decade or longer.

The goal isn't necessarily living to 150. The goal is compressing those years of decline, maintaining vitality until much closer to death. Someone living to 85 but healthy and independent until 83 has a better life than someone living to 90 but dependent from 70 onward.

This is what I think about when I watch my father tend his garden in Garopaba. He's active, engaged, sharp. But I know the actuarial tables, and I know what the typical trajectory looks like from here. The longevity revolution, if it delivers on even a fraction of its promise, could mean the difference between a decade of vitality and a decade of decline. That's not an abstraction. That's my family.

The Economic Impact of Longevity

Longevity isn't only personal. It's economic. If people live longer and healthier, the entire structure of society changes.

Retirement systems strain. Social programs strain. Healthcare costs shift. Work patterns change. Education becomes lifelong. Career paths become multi-phase.

A person may have three careers, multiple reinventions, decades of productive life. This changes how society thinks about age. The automation era may create a world where 60 isn't old, 80 isn't frail, and 100 isn't rare.

Consider retirement systems. Most were designed when life expectancy was lower and the ratio of working-age people to retirees was much higher. As healthspan extends, current retirement ages become economically unsustainable under old assumptions. But extended healthspan also means extended productivity. Someone healthy and sharp at 75 could continue contributing, working part-time, mentoring, volunteering, creating. The economic and social value of an active, healthy older population is enormous.

The Inequality Risk: Biological Stratification

Now we must confront the uncomfortable risk. Longevity could widen inequality. Not only in wealth, but in biology.

If advanced medicine is expensive at first, the wealthy may access it earlier. They live longer. Stay healthier. Accumulate more wealth. Gain more advantage.

This creates biological stratification: a society where the wealthy live longer and the poor age faster. This is one of the darkest possibilities of the longevity revolution. Because it would create a caste system not only of money, but of lifespan.

We already see health inequality. Life expectancy varies dramatically by income and geography. In wealthy countries, the gap in life expectancy between the richest and poorest segments of the population can be a decade or more. Wealthy neighborhoods have better healthcare access, healthier food options, safer environments, less stress.

If AI medicine initially serves primarily wealthy patients who can afford cutting-edge treatments, this gap could widen. The wealthy get personalized cancer treatment, predictive monitoring, optimized longevity interventions. The poor get standard care. Lifespans diverge further.

But this isn't inevitable. Policy can ensure broad access. Public health systems can adopt AI tools. Generic versions of treatments can become available. And some AI-driven advances, like better diagnostic screening, are inherently cheaper to scale than traditional treatments. The question is whether societies choose to democratize longevity advances or allow them to concentrate among the already-privileged.

Longevity and the Purpose Problem

If life becomes longer, purpose becomes more important. Because a longer life requires meaning that lasts.

In the industrial era, life was structured: education, career, retirement, decline. In the longevity era, this structure breaks. If you live to 100 in good health, what is retirement? What is "old age"? What is the narrative of a life?

The longevity revolution forces society to redesign life stages. And redesigning life stages isn't trivial, because life stages provide identity, structure, and meaning.

A longer life without redesigned meaning could become a longer drift. This is why longevity intensifies the purpose problem.

The Psychological Shock of Longer Life

Many people assume longer life is automatically good. It is. But it also creates psychological challenges.

If you live longer, you must face longer relationships, longer responsibilities, longer identity evolution, and longer existential questions. A longer life requires resilience, not only physically, but emotionally. Because you'll experience more change, more reinvention, more loss, and more adaptation.

Longevity is a gift. But it's also a demand. It demands meaning.

The Longevity Revolution as the Final Abundance

If abundance collapses costs and reduces survival anxiety, longevity collapses the greatest scarcity of all: time.

Time is the ultimate scarce resource. A longer, healthier life is the most profound form of abundance. And it changes everything.

Because when humans have more time, they have more opportunity to learn, love, create, serve, and become.

This is the most hopeful vision of the automation era. A world where humans are not only richer, but healthier. Longer-lived. Less burdened by disease. Less burdened by suffering.

This isn't utopia. But it's progress. And progress matters.

When Does This Become Real?

We've explored the forces reshaping robotics, work, income, abundance, globalization, energy, money, education, purpose, and longevity. Now we must ask the question everyone asks:

when does this become real? When does it become visible? When does it reshape daily life?

The future doesn't arrive on a single date. It arrives through adoption. Through phases. Through compounding. The next chapter isn't prophecy. It's a map. A timeline of how the automation era is likely to unfold.

Chapter 16

The Timeline: When the Future Becomes Real

Earlier, I gave you the three-phase framework: Augmentation, Displacement, Compression. Now let's zoom in on what drives the transitions between these phases, why timelines vary by industry and geography, and when specific disruptions become undeniable.

One of the most common questions people ask about the automation era is simple: when?

When will robots be everywhere? When will jobs disappear? When will income systems change? When will abundance be visible? When will the future stop being a concept and start being daily life?

It's a reasonable question. It's also the hardest one.

Because the future doesn't arrive on a single date. It arrives through adoption. Through economics. Through incentives. Through compounding. And compounding has a strange property: it feels slow until it feels fast.

I want to be honest about what I'm doing in this chapter. I'm offering my best assessment of timing, informed by the patterns explored throughout this book, by conversations with people building these technologies, and by my own experience watching digital transformation reshape financial services from the inside. I'm not a prophet. These are educated projections, not predictions. I'll tell you what I think is most likely, what could accelerate it, what could slow it down, and where I could be wrong.

The First Rule: Invention Is Not Adoption

The biggest mistake people make is confusing invention with adoption. A technology can exist for years before it changes society.

Electricity was invented long before it powered every home. Edison's first power plant opened in 1882. But by 1920, nearly forty years later, only about a third of American homes had electricity. Full electrification took until the 1950s.

The internet existed long before it reshaped commerce. The earliest networks launched in the late 1960s. But e-commerce didn't become mainstream until the 2000s, three decades later.

The automation era is the same. AI exists now. Robots exist now. But adoption is what matters. And adoption is driven by economics.

There's a second rule, less obvious but equally important: adoption doesn't move at the same pace everywhere. It moves fastest where incentives are strongest, regulations are lightest, labor is most expensive, and capital is most available.

The automation era will arrive in tech hubs and wealthy nations before it arrives in rural regions and developing economies. Timelines are not global. They're local, sectoral, and deeply uneven.

Phase 1: The Quiet Transformation (Now Through the Late 2020s)

We're already in Phase 1. This phase is defined by AI tools spreading through knowledge work, automation increasing productivity, and robotics expanding in warehouses and logistics.

The economy changes quietly. Companies adopt AI to reduce friction. Some jobs are eliminated. Many jobs are reshaped. But the disruption isn't yet socially explosive.

The concrete markers are already visible. AI coding assistants are becoming standard in software development. Marketing and content teams are shrinking as AI handles generation, scheduling, and analytics. Customer service increasingly relies on AI systems for first-contact resolution. Warehouse robotics expand across logistics networks. Autonomous delivery is appearing in select urban neighborhoods.

Employment effects remain diffuse. Companies hire fewer junior positions but don't announce mass layoffs. The change feels like "efficiency gains" rather than "automation displacement." Underemployment intensifies. Recent graduates discover that entry-level positions are scarcer and expectations are higher.

I see this at Circle. We're a technology company, so we're among the early adopters. The tools our teams use today would have been unrecognizable three years ago. Tasks that required a junior analyst for a week now take a senior person with AI assistance an afternoon. We haven't had dramatic layoffs. But hiring has changed. The roles we're filling require more judgment and less execution. The ladder's lower rungs are getting thinner. And if it's happening in our relatively small company, I know it's happening everywhere.

This ambiguity matters. It allows governments to delay hard decisions. It allows companies to avoid uncomfortable conversations. It allows individuals to believe their specific job is safe. Phase 1 is the window when preparation is cheapest and most effective, and when it's most likely to be avoided.

Phase 2: The Visible Disruption (Late 2020s Through the Mid-2030s)

Phase 2 is when the automation era becomes undeniable. The key shift is visibility: the public begins to see automation in ways that are impossible to explain away.

Driverless vehicles become common in certain regions. Autonomous trucking expands on major freight corridors. Retail logistics becomes automated. Healthcare becomes AI-assisted at scale. This is where the workforce unraveling becomes politically explosive.

Autonomous trucks operating commercially on major freight routes. Robotaxis operating in dozens of major cities. Large retail and fast-food chains deploying automation that visibly reduces staffing. AI handling routine medical diagnostics as standard of care. Law firms and accounting firms hiring significantly fewer new graduates.

The "suddenly" moment likely occurs during Phase 2. Public awareness crystallizes. Media coverage intensifies. Political movements emerge. The narrative shifts from "Is automation happening?" to "How do we handle it?"

This is also when the Ladder Problem becomes impossible to ignore. Not just for economists, but for parents watching their children struggle to find first jobs, for mid-career workers discovering their skills have been devalued, for communities watching local industries hollow out without replacement.

Phase 3: The Social Redesign (Mid-2030s Through the Mid-2040s)

Phase 3 is where society begins to redesign itself. Not because politicians become wise, but because instability forces action.

We'll likely see expanded social income systems, new forms of redistribution, redesigned education, and new cultural institutions for purpose. The wage system is no longer sufficient as the primary distribution mechanism. Different nations will experiment differently, and those experiments will diverge sharply.

Several developed nations pilot or implement universal basic income or Citizens' Dividend programs. Education restructures away from credential-based pathways toward skill and project-based models with AI tutoring. New social institutions emerge: learning guilds, civic service programs, community contribution frameworks.

Healthcare becomes primarily preventive. Continuous monitoring enables early intervention at scale. Life expectancy begins noticeably increasing in developed nations. The economic implications of longer working lives begin reshaping retirement systems.

The culture wars around work, purpose, and identity intensify before they begin to resolve.

Three Scenarios: Conservative, Base, and Acceleration

Any honest discussion of timelines must acknowledge that the future contains genuine uncertainty. The phases above represent a base case, the most probable path given current trajectories. But reasonable scenarios exist that are both slower and faster.

The conservative scenario delays phase shifts by several years. Physical robotics deployment proves slower and harder than anticipated. Humanoid robots remain expensive and limited in real-world dexterity through the early 2030s. Autonomous vehicles face persistent regulatory, legal, and technical obstacles that delay mass deployment. AI capability growth continues but plateaus in certain domains. Labor displacement remains gradual enough that existing social programs absorb the disruption without major redesign.

In this scenario, Phase 1 stretches through the mid-2030s. Phase 2 runs through the mid-2040s. Phase 3 doesn't meaningfully begin until the late 2040s. By 2035, the world looks different but not unrecognizable. Many jobs have changed. Fewer have disappeared. The conversation about income redesign is urgent but not yet forced.

The base scenario is the framework described throughout this book. AI capability continues advancing at roughly current rates. Physical robotics reaches economic viability for a broad range of tasks by the late 2020s. Autonomous vehicles achieve meaningful commercial deployment in favorable geographies by the early 2030s. The Ladder Problem becomes politically visible shortly after. Income distribution debates dominate politics in developed nations by the mid-2030s.

By 2035, the automation era is undeniable. By 2045, social systems in leading nations have been substantially redesigned. The transition is disruptive but manageable for nations that prepared. Devastating for those that didn't.

The acceleration scenario advances phase shifts by a few years. A breakthrough in robotic dexterity, energy density, or AI reasoning capability arrives faster than expected. Humanoid robots reach economic viability at scale by the late 2020s. Autonomous vehicles achieve regulatory approval in major markets around the same time. AI systems begin displacing knowledge workers at rates that produce visible unemployment spikes, not just underemployment.

In the acceleration scenario, Phase 2 arrives before institutions are prepared. The political response is reactive and chaotic. Some nations impose automation taxes or deployment moratoria. Others accelerate. The "suddenly" moment arrives before societies that were counting on a decade to prepare discover they have only years.

The acceleration scenario isn't the most probable outcome. But it isn't implausible. And it's the scenario that argues most strongly for preparing now rather than later.

Signals That Would Accelerate the Timeline

Timelines aren't fixed. They respond to conditions. Certain developments would signal that the acceleration scenario is unfolding:

If humanoid robot costs drop to the point where mid-sized businesses, not just large corporations, can deploy them economically, adoption shifts from linear to exponential. The market expands from hundreds of buyers to millions.

If autonomous trucking achieves regulatory approval across multiple major jurisdictions simultaneously, it signals that the regulatory dam has broken. The freight network is national and international. Approval in enough places effectively means widespread deployment begins.

If a major company announces it is reducing its human workforce by more than twenty percent while maintaining or growing output, it crystallizes public understanding in a way that thousands of smaller displacement events haven't. That announcement becomes the "suddenly" moment.

If an AI system achieves consistent, verifiable performance above human expert level in a licensed profession and regulatory bodies begin adjusting licensing frameworks in response, it signals that even the "safe" high-skill professions are not protected. This accelerates both displacement and the political pressure for income system redesign.

If a significant nation implements a Citizens' Dividend or universal basic income at scale and reports positive early results, policy adoption becomes contagious. One credible large-scale success creates permission for others.

If energy costs for compute drop dramatically in a short period, whether through fusion progress, next-generation solar, or grid modernization, it removes a key bottleneck and allows AI capability to scale faster than current projections assume.

Signals That Would Delay the Timeline

Equally important is knowing what would indicate the conservative scenario is playing out:

If humanoid robots fail to demonstrate reliable dexterity in unstructured, real-world environments by the late 2020s, the physical automation wave arrives later than anticipated. Laboratory demonstrations and actual deployment in messy homes, restaurants, and construction sites are very different things.

If a major autonomous vehicle incident triggers global regulatory retrenchment, deployment could be delayed by years. Public trust in autonomous systems is fragile and has not yet been fully established.

If AI capability growth plateaus in reasoning and planning tasks, the displacement of knowledge workers slows significantly. Current large language models are impressive but have known limitations. If those limitations prove harder to overcome than current trajectories suggest, the timeline extends.

If geopolitical fragmentation produces competing, incompatible AI ecosystems, global adoption slows. Standards wars have historically delayed technology deployment by a decade or more.

If political backlash produces significant automation taxes or deployment moratoria in major economies, corporate adoption slows. This wouldn't stop automation, but it could add years to deployment timelines in affected jurisdictions.

If capital markets reverse course on AI investment, physical deployment slows even if software capabilities continue advancing. The current wave of automation is partly funded by historically elevated investor enthusiasm. A sustained correction would have real effects.

Industry-by-Industry Timing

The automation era doesn't arrive uniformly across industries. It moves fastest where margins are thinnest, labor costs are highest, tasks are most repetitive, and capital is most available.

The first wave, already underway, hits warehousing and logistics, software development, content creation, customer service, and financial analysis. These are domains where AI tools already deliver clear economic value and are being deployed at scale.

The second wave hits transportation, retail, basic medical diagnostics, legal research, and accounting. These require either physical robotics reaching viability or AI systems achieving regulatory acceptance in licensed professions.

The third wave hits construction, complex healthcare, education, skilled trades, and personal services. These require either dramatically more capable physical robotics or fundamental changes in how society certifies and values human work.

Some industries will resist automation longer than economics alone would predict, because human preference demands it. People may choose a human therapist over an AI one even if the AI is statistically more effective. People may prefer human teachers for their children even knowing AI tutors produce better test scores. Human contact carries value that can't be fully automated away. But these preferences come at a price premium, and not everyone can pay it.

The Longevity Timeline

The automation era also reshapes the timeline of human life itself. It's worth placing longevity milestones within the same phase framework.

In Phase 1, AI-enhanced cancer screening begins becoming standard of care in leading health systems. Continuous health monitoring via wearables becomes widespread. Personalized medicine shows measurable early improvements for conditions like diabetes, cardiovascular disease, and certain cancers.

In Phase 2, drug discovery timelines compress significantly as AI systems accelerate the identification and testing of drug candidates. Preventive interventions reduce mortality rates for the leading causes of premature death. Average healthspan in developed nations begins increasing noticeably.

In Phase 3, biological aging interventions move from research to early clinical practice. The concept of "healthy 80" becomes as common as "healthy 60" is today. The social implications of significantly longer lives for marriage, career, identity, and intergenerational wealth begin reshaping culture in ways we can only partially anticipate.

What Would Change My Mind

I want to be honest about the limits of this framework. I've laid out a base case and bracketed it with conservative and acceleration scenarios. But I hold these views with genuine uncertainty. Here is what would cause me to substantially revise them.

I would move toward the conservative scenario if physical robotics proves dramatically harder than anticipated in unstructured real-world environments. The laboratory-to-deployment gap in robotics has historically been enormous. If the next five years show humanoid and service robots struggling with the messy variability of actual human environments, I would revise my timeline for physical automation significantly later.

I would move toward the acceleration scenario if we see a sudden, discontinuous jump in AI reasoning capability, something that crosses from impressive pattern matching to genuine causal reasoning and planning. The history of AI contains occasional step-changes that surprised nearly everyone. If the next step-change arrives sooner than expected, the displacement of knowledge workers would accelerate dramatically faster than my base case assumes.

I would revise my views on policy responses if a major nation implements income support at scale and it either works dramatically better or dramatically worse than predicted. Policy uncertainty is one of the greatest unknowns in this framework.

And I would revise downward my confidence in the entire framework if AI capability growth plateaus significantly in the next few years. Every phase of this analysis assumes continued progress. If that progress stalls, and history shows that progress is not linear, with periods of rapid advance followed by winters of stagnation, the timeline extends substantially, and the urgency of preparation decreases.

I'm not offering these caveats to hedge every claim into meaninglessness. I believe the base case is the most likely path. But intellectual honesty requires acknowledging that the future has always been capable of surprising even careful observers.

The Most Important Timeline: Culture

Technology adoption is fast. Cultural adaptation is slow. The economy can change in a decade. Culture can take generations.

This is why the automation era is dangerous. Technology may outpace meaning. Society may become abundant before it becomes wise. People may have more time before they know what to do with it.

Cultural adaptation cannot be scheduled. But patterns seem likely: initial resistance and denial, followed by experimentation with new models, generational differences in adaptation, and gradual redefinition of what counts as contribution, success, and a good life.

The culture that emerges will depend heavily on choices made during Phase 2, when disruption is undeniable but redesign is still possible. If societies build dignified distribution systems and invest in institutions that support meaning and community, culture adapts constructively. If they don't, culture fractures along lines of purpose and identity, not just income.

I think about this as a father. It was Lila who asked the question at the dinner table that started this book. By the time Phase 2 is fully underway, she'll be old enough to feel its consequences directly. The cultural script I was given, study hard, get a good job, work your way up, may not apply to her generation at all. She asked what happens when robots do everything. I wrote a book trying to answer. But the honest truth is that the answer depends less on technology than on the cultural choices her generation inherits. I don't know yet what those will be. But I know they matter more than almost any technology question in this book.

The "Suddenly" Moment

Every major transition has a "suddenly" moment. A point where society realizes the old assumptions no longer hold.

For the automation era, that moment may be the widespread visibility of driverless vehicles in everyday life. It may be a high-profile announcement by a major company of dramatic workforce reduction. It may be a political crisis triggered by distribution tension. It may be a generation of young adults struggling collectively and visibly to find first jobs.

The "suddenly" moment is when the automation era becomes undeniable. And once it's undeniable, redesign accelerates. Because denial is no longer possible. The question that was theoretical becomes urgent. The policies that seemed premature become necessary.

We don't know exactly when that moment arrives. But we know it's coming. The question isn't whether to prepare. It's whether we prepare before the moment or in response to it. Before is cheaper. Before preserves choices. Before allows design rather than reaction.

The Uneven Future

The automation era will not create one future. It will create many futures unfolding simultaneously. Some regions will become abundant, automated, and stable. Others will become disrupted, unstable, and polarized. The same technology that generates prosperity in one place will generate upheaval in another, depending on institutions, governance, capital access, and the choices societies make now, in the window we are in.

This unevenness will shape migration, geopolitics, and global tension for decades. The automation era won't be a smooth transition. It will be messy. But messiness doesn't mean failure. It means humanity is adapting. And adaptation, even when painful, has always been what humans do best.

What Comes After the Timeline

We've mapped the forces. We've mapped the phases. We've bracketed the uncertainty. Now we arrive at the final question.

Not when. Not how fast.

Is the future good?

Not guaranteed. But possible.

The automation era is a fork. One path leads to abundance and dignity. The other leads to abundance and instability. The difference isn't technology. It's wisdom. It's governance. It's the cultural choices societies make about who deserves what, and what a life well-lived looks like when survival is no longer the point.

The final chapter isn't naive optimism. It's strategic optimism. Because pessimism is easy, and despair is comfortable. But designing a good future is hard.

That's what we explore next.

Chapter 17
The Best Possible Future

There's a reason so many conversations about the future feel dark.

Fear is compelling. Dystopia is entertaining. Collapse is dramatic. Optimism can sound naive.

And the automation era contains real risks: job disruption, inequality, political instability, loss of purpose, surveillance, concentration of power, a widening global divide. These risks are real. They deserve seriousness.

But seriousness is not the same as despair.

I want to tell you something about how this book nearly ended differently. Around Chapter 10, somewhere deep in the geopolitics of the automation divide, I hit a wall. Not a writing wall. A psychological one. I'd spent months staring at the logic of displacement, of labor markets unraveling, of entire nations falling behind, and I started to wonder whether I was writing a warning or an obituary. Whether the honest conclusion was just: this is going to be very bad for a lot of people, and there's not much anyone can do about it.

I called my wife Laura that night and told her I wasn't sure the book should have a hopeful ending. That maybe hope was dishonest. She listened for a while, the way she does, and then said something simple: "You're not writing this for people who've already given up. You're writing it for people who want to know what to build."

She was right. And this chapter is for those people.

The automation era contains something rare: a chance to reduce human suffering at a scale never before possible. A chance to make the world not only richer but kinder. Not automatically. Not inevitably. But plausibly.

This chapter is about that plausibility. It's about what the best possible future looks like. And what it requires. Because the future is not guaranteed to be good. But it's capable of being extraordinary.

The Automation Era Is a Fork

The automation era is not a single destiny. It's a fork. One path leads to abundance and dignity. The other leads to abundance and instability.

The difference is distribution. The difference is purpose. The difference is governance.

Technology is a multiplier. It amplifies what societies already are. If societies are wise, technology amplifies wisdom. If societies are greedy, technology amplifies greed. If societies are compassionate, technology amplifies compassion.

I've seen this principle operate in miniature throughout my career. At Apple, I watched technology amplify both creative brilliance and corporate ruthlessness, sometimes in the same product cycle. At Facebook, I saw a platform designed for connection become a vehicle for division, not because the engineers were malicious, but because the system amplified whatever humans brought to it. At Circle, I'm watching financial technology either democratize access to the global economy or concentrate it further, depending entirely on the choices made by the people building and regulating it.

The automation era is not a test of engineering. It's a test of civilization.

The Core Vision

Machines can produce wealth. But machines cannot produce meaning. Machines can build. But they cannot love. Machines can optimize. But they cannot belong. Machines can predict. But they cannot care.

The best possible future is one where machines do the work and humans do the living.

The best possible future solves the Ladder Problem not by fixing old ladders but by creating entirely new structures for distributing opportunity and meaning.

This is the core vision of the Age of Abundance. Not a world where humans become lazy. A world where humans become fully human.

The Greatest Benefit: Reducing Suffering

Let's be blunt. Modern life contains unnecessary suffering. Not because humans are evil. Because scarcity is brutal.

People suffer because they can't afford healthcare. Because they can't afford housing. Because they can't access education. Because they're trapped in exhausting work. Because they live with constant financial anxiety.

I didn't grow up wealthy. I grew up in Brazil, where the gap between what life could be and what life actually was hit you every day. You'd drive past a gated condominium and two blocks later pass a favela where families shared a single room. The poverty wasn't hidden. It was right there, separated from comfort by nothing more than a road and the accidents of birth. That proximity shapes you. It makes abstractions like "global poverty statistics" feel obscene, because you know those statistics have faces. They have children who look like your children.

Globally, roughly 700 million people live in extreme poverty. About 2 billion lack adequate healthcare access. Nearly 800 million are chronically hungry. One billion children lack adequate education.

If automation truly collapses costs, food production, basic healthcare, education delivery, shelter construction, these numbers could decline dramatically. Not overnight. Not everywhere simultaneously. But meaningfully.

The reduction of preventable suffering at scale would be one of the greatest achievements in human history. That possibility alone justifies taking the automation era seriously. And it's the reason I kept writing past Chapter 10.

The Abundance Dividend

The best possible future requires a new social contract. Because job income won't remain the default distribution system. The automation era must distribute abundance.

This can take many forms: universal basic income, social dividends, expanded welfare, negative income taxes, public ownership of automation infrastructure, or hybrid systems. Different nations will choose different paths. The key is not ideology. The key is stability.

Alaska provides a real-world model. The Alaska Permanent Fund distributes oil revenue to all residents: roughly $1,000–2,000 annually per person. It's wildly popular across the political spectrum because it's framed as shared ownership of a common resource, not welfare.

The automation dividend could work similarly: automation creates enormous productivity gains. Those gains represent collective benefit from infrastructure, education, and technological progress built over generations. Distributing a portion ensures stability and legitimacy.

Dignity Is Not Optional

Distribution is necessary. But it's not sufficient. The best possible future requires dignity.

Because humans don't only need money. We need respect. We need belonging. We need contribution. A society that provides income but treats citizens as unnecessary will fail. It'll produce resentment, humiliation, anger.

The automation era must honor contribution beyond employment: caregiving, mentorship, community building, art, service, learning, mastery. These must be culturally legitimate. Not treated as hobbies. Not treated as laziness.

Imagine a society where someone spending 30 hours weekly caring for an aging parent receives recognition and support, not invisibility. Someone coaching youth sports, mentoring struggling students, or organizing community gardens is honored for social contribution. Someone pursuing mastery in woodworking, music, or writing is respected for craft, not dismissed as "unemployed."

This requires cultural shift. But culture can change. A century ago, women's suffrage seemed radical. Child labor seemed normal. Segregation seemed inevitable. Each became unthinkable through moral evolution.

The Purpose Renaissance

The most hopeful vision of the automation era isn't leisure. It's purpose.

A world where humans choose work because it's meaningful. A world where art flourishes, caregiving is honored, community is rebuilt, learning becomes lifelong, and mastery becomes central.

This isn't fantasy. It's human nature. Humans aren't designed for endless idleness. We're designed to grow, to build, to serve, to create.

I'll confess something. Writing this book has been the most purposeful experience of my professional life. More than any corporate role, any promotion, any deal I've closed. Not because the book is important, though I hope it is. Because the act of building something from nothing, of wrestling with ideas until they become clear, of sitting alone with a blank page and making it say something true, that process gave me a sense of meaning that no salary ever matched. And the irony is not lost on me: AI tools helped me write a better book. Claude, ChatGPT, Grok, they were collaborators in the truest sense. The human-AI partnership I describe in this book is the one I lived while writing it.

The Renaissance happened partly because patronage freed artists and thinkers from survival concerns. Michelangelo spent years on the Sistine Chapel. Da Vinci pursued diverse interests. The automation era could democratize this pattern at unprecedented scale.

Not everyone becomes Michelangelo. But everyone gets the opportunity to pursue meaningful work rather than merely surviving. That shift, from compulsory labor to chosen purpose, could be the most significant upgrade in the human experience since we stopped being nomads.

The Reinvention of Community

One of the greatest risks of the automation era is isolation. Modern life is already isolating: remote work, digital entertainment, algorithmic feeds. The automation era could intensify this. But it could also reverse it.

If humans have more time, they can invest in community. Local projects. Civic organizations. Sports. Arts. Mentorship. The best possible future isn't one where everyone sits alone with perfect entertainment. It's one where humans rebuild social fabric.

I think about this often when I think about Garopaba, the small town in southern Brazil where I'm building a house and where I plan to live. Garopaba has something that most American suburbs have lost: people actually know each other. They stop to talk on the street. They share meals without scheduling them two weeks in advance. Children play outside without parental surveillance apps. It's not paradise. It has its problems. But the social fabric is intact in a way that feels almost foreign after years in the United States.

The automation era could make more places feel like Garopaba. If people have time, if survival pressure eases, if the frantic pace of modern work slows, communities can rebuild. Not because technology forces connection, but because it finally stops preventing it. The greatest obstacle to community in modern life isn't technology. It's exhaustion. Remove the exhaustion, and humans do what humans have always done: they find each other.

Because belonging is one of the deepest sources of meaning. And meaning is the antidote to the emptiness of abundance.

Longevity as a Gift, Not a Curse

The longevity revolution could be one of the greatest blessings in history. Longer healthspan. Less disease. More vitality. More years with family. More years of learning and contribution.

My dad is in his late seventies now. When I think about what the longevity revolution means, I don't think about statistics. I think about him. About the possibility that breakthroughs in the next decade could give him ten or fifteen additional healthy years. Years where he'll not just be alive but vital. Years where he'll know his grandchildren not as teens but as adults. Years where the retirement he earned isn't a slow decline but an entirely new chapter.

And then I think about Luca and Lila, and what longevity means for a generation that might live past 100. Their lives won't be a single career. They'll be a sequence of reinventions. A series of phases. Multiple identities, multiple callings, multiple communities across a span of time that would have been unimaginable to their great-grandparents.

But longevity also intensifies the purpose problem. A longer life requires meaning that lasts. The best possible future is one where longer life is paired with redesigned life stages, opportunities for reinvention, and cultural permission to evolve.

In the best possible future, a human life isn't a single career. It's a journey. Longevity becomes a canvas, not a burden.

The Global Responsibility

The automation era risks widening the global divide. Wealthy nations adopt faster, become more self-sufficient, reduce dependence on imports. Developing nations lose the cheap-labor ladder.

This is one of the most dangerous outcomes. Because a world of abundance islands surrounded by instability is not stable. The best possible future requires global responsibility. Not out of charity. Out of self-interest. Because instability spreads.

As someone who was born in the developing world and now lives in the developed world, I carry this tension personally. Brazil is not a poor country, but it is an unequal one. And the automation era could widen that inequality catastrophically if the benefits concentrate in nations that already have capital, compute, and energy infrastructure while countries like Brazil fall further behind. Or it could narrow it, if technology transfer, energy investment, and institutional support give developing nations a genuine path into the automated economy. The outcome depends on choices that wealthy nations will make in the next decade. Those choices will determine whether the automation era is remembered as the moment humanity rose together or the moment it fractured permanently.

The automation era must include technology sharing, education support, energy infrastructure investment, and institutional strengthening. Otherwise, the global divide becomes a global crisis.

The Role of Individuals

At this point, it's tempting to place the burden entirely on governments. But individuals matter. Culture is built by people. Purpose is built by people. Community is built by people.

The best possible future isn't only a policy project. It's a human project. It requires citizens who choose contribution over drift, mastery over distraction, community over isolation, and meaning over sedation.

This isn't moralizing. It's survival. A society of distracted, purposeless citizens is easy to control. A society of purposeful, engaged citizens is resilient.

Why Optimism Is Rational

Optimism is often treated as naive. But pessimism isn't intelligence. Pessimism is a mood.

Optimism, in this context, isn't blind hope. It's strategic. Because the automation era creates real potential. Abundance is real. Longevity is real. Education access is real. Suffering reduction is real.

The question isn't whether these benefits exist. It's whether we can design systems to distribute them. This is difficult. But difficulty is not impossibility.

Human history is a story of solving problems. Not perfectly. Not universally. But meaningfully. The automation era is simply the next great problem. And it may be the greatest opportunity.

A Perfect Day in 2045

Let me show you what the best possible future actually feels like. Not as abstract policy. As a Tuesday.

James is 36 years old and lives in Austin, Texas with his partner Sophie and their daughter Mia, who is eight. He works about 22 hours a week as a renewable energy consultant, mostly reviewing AI-generated analyses of solar deployments across Southeast Asia and building relationships with clients who still prefer talking to a human. Sophie trains AI healthcare systems about 16 hours a week. Between their work income and the Citizens' Dividend they both receive, the family is comfortable. Not wealthy. Comfortable.

On this particular Tuesday, James finishes a video call with a client in Vietnam around 11, the conversation translated in real time by AI so seamless that both of them have forgotten it's there. He picks up lunch, meets Sophie, and they eat outside because the weather is good and the robotaxi cost them a dollar twenty each way. After lunch, he goes to a ceramics studio he's been visiting for two years. He is not talented. The AI-driven 3D printers at the shop next door produce objectively better pottery for a fraction of the cost. He doesn't care. The clay is the point. The focus. The hour where nothing matters except the weight of wet earth between his hands.

He picks up Mia at 3:30 from a school that blends AI tutors with human teachers who focus on the things AI cannot teach: empathy, collaboration, the ability to sit with uncertainty. Mia is working on a model city project and wants to explain every detail. They go to the park, which is immaculately maintained by machines, and James listens while she talks about bridges.

Dinner is at home. Sophie cooks because she finds it meditative, not because they couldn't order something delivered in twelve minutes for almost nothing. Mia does homework. They call James's parents, both in their seventies, healthy, traveling, receiving the Dividend plus Social Security, living a retirement that looks nothing like the slow decline their own parents endured. After Mia goes to bed, James works on a piece of pottery in the small studio he's set up in the garage. He'll probably give it away. The value is in the making.

Is this utopia? No. James still has client deadlines that stress him. Sophie still argues with hospital administrators about AI implementation. Mia still has bad days at school. James still sometimes lies awake wondering if his work matters, or if the AI could do it without him, or if the pottery is just a way to avoid thinking about that question too carefully.

But his baseline reality is abundance. Material scarcity is not a constraint. Time scarcity is not a constraint. Survival is guaranteed. His daughter has opportunities he couldn't have imagined at her age. His parents are thriving instead of deteriorating. His life has structure that he chose, not structure imposed by survival necessity. Meaning must be discovered rather than assigned, and that is both the challenge and the gift.

This is the best possible future. Not perfect, but extraordinary. Not without problems, but without the fundamental problem of scarcity. Not guaranteed for everyone, but achievable for most if we design the systems correctly.

This is what the Age of Abundance looks like when it works. This is why the title isn't ironic. This is what we're building toward, if we choose to build it well.

The Age of Abundance

The title of this book is not a marketing trick. It's a claim.

The automation era can produce abundance. Not only wealth: time, health, knowledge, mobility, energy, opportunity.

But abundance is not the final goal. Abundance is the foundation. The final goal is something deeper:

A civilization where survival is not the main story. Where humans are free to pursue meaning. Where suffering is reduced. Where life is longer and healthier. Where dignity is universal.

This is the best possible future. It's not guaranteed. But it's available. And that availability is the most important fact of our time.

A Final Thought

There will be fear. There will be turbulence. There will be political conflict. There will be mistakes. There will be winners and losers. There will be moments when the future feels unstable.

But beneath the turbulence, something profound is happening.

Human beings are building machines that can produce abundance. For the first time in history, it's plausible that food scarcity declines dramatically, disease burden falls, education becomes universal, and survival anxiety weakens.

This isn't utopia. But it's extraordinary. And it deserves courage.

Because the automation era is not asking whether we can

build machines. We can. It's asking whether we can build a society worthy of what we're creating.

I started this book because my daughter asked a question at the dinner table that I couldn't stop thinking about. I'm finishing it because I want her, and Luca, and every kid growing up right now, to inherit a world where that question leads somewhere good. Where the machines do the work. Where the humans do the living. Where the abundance is shared. Where the meaning is real.

That is the challenge. That is the test. And that is the opportunity.

The future is not guaranteed to be good. But it's capable of being extraordinary.

And that, perhaps, is the most hopeful sentence of the century.

Chapter 18

Positioning for the Shift

I want to tell you about a conversation I had with a friend over dinner last year.

He'd read an early draft of several chapters. He understood the argument. He understood the timeline. He understood the economic logic. He sat quietly for a minute, then said something that stuck with me: "Okay. I believe you. Now what am I supposed to do with this?"

It was the most honest question anyone had asked me about this book. Because understanding what's coming and knowing how to position yourself within it are two very different things.

This chapter isn't a financial plan. It's not a career guide. It's not a ten-step program. Those would require knowing your specific circumstances, and I don't. What I can offer is something more foundational: a way of thinking about personal positioning when the entire economic structure is shifting beneath your feet.

Because the automation era isn't something you watch from the stands. You're already in the game. The question is whether you're playing with intention or being moved by forces you haven't yet noticed.

Think Like the Book, Not Like the Headlines

Most public conversation about AI operates at the surface. Will this job disappear? Will that company dominate? Is this technology overhyped? Those are tactical questions. They matter. But they're not foundational.

The foundational questions are the ones we've been exploring throughout this book. How is the cost of effort changing? How is value migrating from labor toward capital? Where is energy infrastructure strengthening? How is money evolving?

When you internalize those structural shifts, something changes in how you process information. You stop reacting to every headline about a new AI model or a company layoff. You start recognizing patterns. You start anticipating incentives. And incentives, over long horizons, shape everything.

Let me give you a concrete example. In early 2025, a wave of tech layoffs dominated the news cycle. People panicked. Commentators declared the tech boom was over. But if you understood the structural logic, that companies were replacing headcount with AI capabilities, not shrinking, you saw something different. You saw firms becoming more productive with fewer people. You saw the economics of labor shifting in real time. You saw the thesis of this book playing out in quarterly earnings reports.

That's the difference between reactive thinking and structural thinking. Reactive thinking says: layoffs are bad, the economy must be weakening. Structural thinking says: layoffs alongside rising revenue and productivity means the labor equation is changing permanently. Both see the same data. One understands what it means.

The Ownership Imperative

If you take one thing from this book, let it be this: the automation era rewards ownership.

This isn't ideology. This is arithmetic. When production becomes capital-intensive rather than labor-intensive, when the factory runs on robots, the office runs on AI, the logistics chain runs on autonomous systems, the returns flow to whoever owns the productive infrastructure. Not to whoever operates it. The operators are being replaced. That's the entire point.

For most of the twentieth century, a middle-class person could participate in economic growth primarily through wages. You got a job, your wages grew roughly in line with productivity, and that was how you captured your share of the expanding economy. Chapter 5 explained why that arrangement is breaking down. The share of economic output going to labor has been declining for decades, and automation accelerates that trend.

This means participation in ownership becomes structurally important in a way it hasn't been for most people in most of history.

Ownership of what? Productive systems. Capital. Equity in companies deploying automation. Energy infrastructure. Real assets. Intellectual property. The specifics depend on individual circumstances, risk tolerance, and opportunity. But the principle is universal: if labor's share of economic output declines, you want to be positioned on the capital side of the ledger, not exclusively on the labor side.

I learned this lesson viscerally, not from economics textbooks, but from watching my parents navigate Brazil's economic chaos in the 1980s and 1990s. Hyperinflation destroyed the value of wages overnight. People who held only cash or salary income watched their purchasing power evaporate. People who owned real assets, property, businesses, hard goods, survived. The lesson was burned into me: income is a stream. Ownership is a foundation. The automation era is creating a different kind of erosion than hyperinflation, but the structural principle is the same. When the floor shifts, you want to be standing on something you own.

I'm not offering investment advice. I'm describing a structural reality. Over long time horizons, compounding returns on capital will likely outpace wage growth more dramatically than at any previous point in modern history. Understanding that shift allows intentional positioning rather than accidental exposure.

And here's the part that matters most: this isn't only relevant for wealthy people. A twenty-five-year-old contributing to a retirement account that holds broadly diversified equity is participating in ownership. A small business owner investing in automation tools for their own operation is participating in ownership. A freelancer building intellectual property rather than billing exclusively for hours is participating in ownership. The forms vary. The principle doesn't.

Adaptability as Strategy

A friend of mine manages a team of software engineers. Three years ago, his team had twelve developers. Today, the same output is produced by seven, with AI handling much of the routine work. The five who left weren't fired. They were absorbed elsewhere, or they moved on. But here's what my friend noticed: the developers who thrived weren't necessarily the most technically brilliant. They were the ones who adapted fastest. Who learned to collaborate with AI tools rather than compete against them. Who treated each new capability as an expansion of their own capacity rather than a threat to their relevance.

That pattern will repeat across virtually every profession.

The automation era rewards adaptability. Industries will compress. New opportunities will emerge in places nobody currently predicts. Career arcs will evolve in ways that make the traditional résumé look quaint. The most resilient people won't be those who cling to the way things were. They'll be those who understand how to work alongside systems that are changing rapidly.

Investing in adaptability means investing intellectually: staying curious, learning continuously, building skills that complement rather than compete with automation. It means investing emotionally: developing the psychological resilience to handle disruption without spiraling into fear or paralysis. And it means investing practically: building financial buffers that give you the freedom to pivot when pivoting becomes necessary.

Adaptability creates optionality. Optionality reduces fear. And fear, more than any technological disruption, is what narrows judgment and leads to bad decisions during transitions.

Follow the Energy

Chapter 11 made the case that energy is destiny in the automation era. That argument has personal implications that most people overlook.

Energy isn't abstract. It's geographical. It's economic. It's strategic. Regions with abundant, stable, affordable energy will accelerate. Their economies will attract capital, deploy automation faster, and create new opportunities earlier. Regions without energy infrastructure will lag. Sometimes dramatically.

This matters for where you live, where you invest, and where you see long-term economic vitality. States and countries with large energy grids and favorable business environments look structurally different from those wrestling with energy constraints. Nations investing commodity wealth into renewable infrastructure and AI capacity look structurally different from those dependent on exports with no transition plan.

I'm making a personal bet on this thesis. The house I'm building in Garopaba isn't just a family home. It's a bet on Brazil's energy future. Brazil has extraordinary hydroelectric capacity, growing solar potential, and the kind of energy abundance that the automation era rewards. If the institutional framework keeps improving, Brazil could be one of the surprising winners of this transition. That's not a guarantee. Brazil has a long history of squandering structural advantages through governance failures. But the energy foundation is real, and I'm positioning around it.

You don't need to become an energy analyst. But understanding where infrastructure is strengthening, geographically and economically, informs long-term planning in ways that most people don't consider. Infrastructure decisions outlast headlines. They shape decades.

The Money Layer

Chapter 12 explored how money itself is changing. That has practical implications too.

The automation era will likely accelerate the shift from analog to programmable money. Stablecoins, central bank digital currencies, and real-time payment systems are already reshaping how value moves. Understanding this shift matters because financial infrastructure is the plumbing of the economy. When the plumbing changes, everything built on top of it changes too.

I work at Circle. I've spent years watching this infrastructure get built. So I'm biased, and I want to be transparent about that. But I'm also informed by proximity. What I can tell you is that the speed at which digital financial infrastructure is being adopted, particularly outside the United States, is faster than most people in traditional finance appreciate. Populations that were excluded from the old financial system are building their economic lives on the new one. That's not a trend that reverses.

For individuals, the practical implication is straightforward: understand how money is evolving. Not to speculate on any particular token or platform, but because the financial tools available to you in five years will look very different from the ones available today. People who understand programmable money, digital assets, and decentralized finance will have options that others won't. Literacy in the new financial system is a form of positioning.

The Most Valuable Asset

Here's a sentence that would have made no sense fifty years ago: time is becoming the ultimate strategic asset.

Automation expands productive capacity. Longevity extends lifespan. Together, they create a world where time is both more abundant and more valuable. You will likely have more years of healthy life than any previous generation. The question becomes what you do with them.

Without intention, expanded time dissipates into distraction. The comfort trap from Chapter 14 is real. Infinite entertainment, algorithmically optimized to capture attention, is extraordinarily good at consuming hours that could have been invested in something that compounds.

With intention, time compounds into contribution. Learning compounds. Relationships compound. Health compounds. Creative work compounds. Building things, businesses, skills, communities, families, compounds over decades in ways that are almost impossible to appreciate in the moment.

Protecting time for learning, reflection, health, and meaningful work isn't indulgent. In the Age of Abundance, it's strategic. The people who treat their time as their most valuable resource, who guard it against low-value consumption and direct it toward high-value creation, will be positioned fundamentally differently from those who let it slip away.

Choose Your Purpose Before It Chooses You

Chapter 14 explored the purpose problem in depth. But the purpose problem isn't only a societal challenge. It's a personal one. And it arrives sooner than most people expect.

If work becomes less tied to survival, and the trajectory of this book suggests it will, then purpose must be chosen consciously. Not assigned by an employer. Not inherited from cultural expectation. Not defaulted into through inertia. Chosen.

I've watched people struggle with this. A colleague who retired early with more than enough money and spent three years feeling lost before discovering that mentoring young professionals gave him more satisfaction than any salary ever had. A family member who defined herself entirely through her career and felt like a stranger in her own life when the career ended.

The people who navigate this best are those who build purpose before they need it. Who invest in creative work, family, community engagement, mastery of a craft, service to others, not as hobbies squeezed into weekends, but as genuine pillars of identity. In a world of expanding optionality, clarity of purpose becomes a source of strength. Without it, optionality becomes paralyzing.

Lila is thirteen now, the one who asked the dinner table question that started this entire project. She's three years older and already more aware of how fast things are changing. Luca is sixteen, planning for medicine but curious about everything. They'll both enter the workforce during the years this book describes as the most disruptive. I don't give them the same advice my parents gave me, because the world won't reward the same things. What I tell them is simpler and harder: figure out what you care about deeply enough to sustain you when the external structures shift. Build around that. The structures will shift. What you've built inside won't.

Design your purpose. Don't wait for institutions to hand it to you. Whether it's entrepreneurship, creative work, raising a family with deep intention, civic engagement, research, mentorship, or mastery of something you care about, direction stabilizes identity when everything else is shifting.

Expecting the Turbulence

I want to be honest about something. The transition we've described in this book will not unfold smoothly. It never does.

Markets will fluctuate, sometimes violently. Public discourse will polarize around automation, around AI, around the future of work, around distribution. Policy will lag behind technology, as it always does. Breakthroughs will surprise everyone, including the experts. There will be recessions, political upheavals, industry collapses, and moments when the entire thesis of this book seems wrong.

Volatility is not evidence of failure. It's evidence of transition. Every major structural shift in economic history, industrialization, electrification, the computer revolution, produced turbulence, fear, political conflict, and real hardship before the new equilibrium emerged.

I grew up in a country defined by turbulence. Brazil in the 1980s and 1990s was a masterclass in what happens when economic structures shift faster than institutions can adapt. Hyperinflation. Currency changes. Savings wiped out overnight. My parents navigated it by staying anchored to fundamentals: real assets, real skills, real relationships. The specific chaos was unpredictable. The principle of anchoring to fundamentals was not. The automation era will produce its own turbulence. The principle holds.

Planning for continuity through volatility requires long-term thinking. It requires anchoring to structural direction rather than short-term noise. It requires building financial resilience, reserves, diversified income, manageable debt, that lets you absorb shocks without making panicked decisions. And it requires the psychological steadiness to distinguish between a bad quarter and a broken thesis.

The structural direction of the automation era is clear, even when the daily headlines are chaotic. Labor becomes less central to production. Capital intensity increases. Energy becomes foundational. Finance accelerates. Longevity extends. Purpose must be intentional. If you anchor to those realities, the turbulence becomes navigable. Not comfortable. But navigable.

The Long View

The automation era can feel threatening if viewed through a narrow lens. My job. My industry. My assumptions about how the world works. Seen that way, the disruption feels personal. Feels targeted. Feels like loss.

But pull back, and the picture changes.

Human history is a story of expanding capacity. Fire. Agriculture. Industry. Electricity. Computing. Each transformation disrupted the existing order. Each also expanded what was possible. The automation era is larger in scope than any previous transition. But it follows the same underlying principle: when the cost of effort declines, civilization reorganizes around new possibilities.

Reorganization is uncomfortable. I've never argued otherwise. But it is also creative. The automation era doesn't only eliminate old patterns. It enables new ones. New forms of work. New kinds of contribution. New ways of living. New expressions of what it means to be human when survival is no longer the central occupation.

That's the long view. And the long view matters because it determines whether you approach this transition with fear or with clarity. Fear narrows your options. Clarity expands them.

Design, Don't Drift

The Age of Abundance is not guaranteed. It's possible. And possibility requires intention.

At the personal level, that means designing your positioning thoughtfully. Understanding ownership. Building adaptability. Following energy. Protecting time. Choosing purpose. Expecting volatility. Maintaining perspective.

At the institutional level, and this matters too, because individuals shape institutions, it means advocating for policies that expand ownership, strengthen energy resilience, modernize education, reform financial systems, and ensure that the abundance created by automation reaches broadly rather than concentrating narrowly.

Drift produces concentration. Design produces participation. This is true at every scale, from national policy to personal decisions.

You don't need to predict every technological breakthrough. You don't need to time every inflection point. You don't need to be right about whether full automation arrives in 2035 or 2045. You need only understand the structural direction. Automation reduces the marginal necessity of labor. Capital intensity increases. Energy becomes foundational. Finance accelerates. Longevity expands time. Purpose must be intentional.

If you anchor your decisions around those realities, you won't be surprised by the transition. You'll be positioned within it.

The Age of Abundance won't arrive as an announcement. It will accumulate. Quietly. Persistently. Through a thousand rational decisions made in conference rooms and living rooms and legislatures and laboratories.

And your advantage won't come from reacting to it late. It will come from understanding it early.

Which, if you've read this far, you already do.

The future is not something that happens to you. It's something you prepare for. And preparation begins with clarity.

You have the clarity now. The rest is up to you.

What You Can Do Now

You've just finished reading about the most significant economic transformation in human history. The Age of Abundance is coming, whether we design it well or poorly is up to us.

This isn't about agreeing with every prediction in this book. It's about recognizing that the conversation matters and participating in it.

Here's how you can engage:

1. Join the Conversation

I publish regular updates exploring these ideas in depth, responding to reader questions, and tracking how the automation era unfolds in real time.

Sign up for updates at: www.leandromaya.com

Connect on LinkedIn: linkedin.com/in/leandromaya

2. Share This Book

If this book changed how you think about the future, share it. Post about The Ladder Problem on social media. Recommend it to colleagues wrestling with career uncertainty. Gift it to someone facing automation anxiety. Ideas spread through conversation.

3. Leave an Honest Review

Reviews help other readers discover this book. If you found it valuable, or if you disagreed with parts, leave a review on Amazon or Goodreads. Your perspective helps refine the conversation.

4. Engage with Your Community

Talk about these ideas with your family, your workplace, your professional network. The automation era requires collective problem-solving. Start those conversations now.

If you'd like to continue the conversation, you can reach me directly at hello@leandromaya.com

A Final Thought

The future isn't predetermined. The automation era offers humanity a choice: we can design systems that distribute abundance broadly, or we can allow it to concentrate among a small elite while others struggle.

The Ladder Problem is solvable. The distribution crisis has solutions. The best possible future is achievable.

But only if we choose to build it.

Thank you for reading. Now let's get to work.

— Leandro Maya

February 2026

About the Author

Leandro Maya is a finance professional, entrepreneur, and investor passionate about the forces reshaping the future of human life. His career has spanned major technology companies including Apple, Facebook, and Circle, where he gained firsthand insight into how innovation transforms industries and economies. This experience in both finance and the technology sector gives him a unique perspective on the intersection of automation, markets, and human systems.

In The Age of Abundance: AI and the Future of Work, Wealth, and Purpose, Leandro offers a clear, optimistic, and deeply human exploration of what happens when machines begin to replace both labor and cognition at scale. He examines the disruption of the workforce, the redesign of social programs, the collapse of costs through extreme efficiency, the shifting balance between nations, and the coming revolution in medicine and longevity. Above all, he argues that the greatest challenge of the automation era will not be technological, but psychological: how human beings find meaning and purpose in a world where survival no longer requires work.

Drawing on his professional experience across finance and technology, Leandro brings a practical, economically grounded perspective to questions often dominated by either techno-utopianism or dystopian fear. He writes with the belief that the future is not guaranteed to be good, but it is capable of being extraordinary.

Connect with Leandro:

Newsletter: www.leandromaya.com/newsletter

LinkedIn: linkedin.com/in/leandromaya

Email: hello@leandromaya.com

Also By Leandro Maya

THE AGE OF ABUNDANCE SERIES

A series exploring how AI and automation are reshaping civilization's core systems. Each book stands alone. Together, they map what comes next.

Available Now:

The Age of Abundance: AI and the Future of Work, Wealth, and Purpose

Next in the Series:

The Ladder Problem: Work in the Age of Abundance

When automation eliminates entry-level jobs, the entire economic ladder breaks. Not at the top, at the bottom. This book is a deep dive into the structural crisis that emerges when the path from education to employment to stability loses its first rungs.

The Invisible Team: Entrepreneurship in the Age of Abundance

AI agents can now perform the work of lawyers, accountants, marketers, and engineers at a fraction of the cost. This book explores what it means for economies and opportunity when anyone can build something that competes at scale.

The Decoupling: Money in the Age of Abundance

When labor income collapses but asset values soar, the financial system must evolve or break. This book explores how money, banking, and wealth distribution transform when the link between work and income dissolves.

The Unretirement: Longevity and Retirement in the Age of Abundance

What happens when people live to 100 but traditional careers end at 45? Social Security was designed for a world where people worked until 65 and died at 72. That world is gone.

The Obsolete Degree: Education in the Age of Abundance

For decades, the deal was simple: earn a degree, get a job. That deal is breaking. This book argues that education must stop preparing students to climb a ladder that no longer exists.

The Purpose Crisis: Meaning in the Age of Abundance

The final book in the series, and the hardest question. When material comfort is guaranteed and survival is assured, what gives life meaning?

Abundance is achievable.

Whether we build it well is up to us.

For updates on new releases and to join the conversation:

Website: www.leandromaya.com

Linkedin: www.linkedin.com/in/leandromaya

Email: hello@leandromaya.com